MW01517832

Ten Things You Need to Know

Before You Interview for a

Teaching Job

Ten Things You Need to Know
Before You Interview for a Teaching Job

Dr. Nancy Maynes

and

Dr. Glynn Sharpe

Library of Congress Control Number: 2013915951
ISBN: Hardcover   978-1-4836-9383-5
               Softcover   978-1-4836-9382-8
               Ebook   978-1-4836-9384-2

This book was printed in the United States of America.

Rev. date: 09/17/2013

To order additional copies of this book, contact:
Xlibris LLC
1-888-795-4274
www.Xlibris.com
Orders@Xlibris.com
141448

CONTENTS

Chapter 1: Introduction/Context.. 11

Chapter 2: Know the Process: Applying for a
Teaching Position.. 15

Chapter 3: Get Your Paper Work in Order to Help you
Stand Out: Your Resume and Supporting
Documentation 19

Chapter 4: Dress for the Role 49

Chapter 5: Knowing Who will Interview You.......................... 55

Chapter 6: Read the Room: You Only Have One Chance
to Make a Good First Impression!........................... 67

Chapter 7: Know how Interviews are Structured:
Expecting the Style of Questions you may Get............ 76

Chapter 8: Anticipate the Questions 87

Chapter 9: Structure Your Responses.. 96

Chapter 10: Take Control of the Closing of Your Interview 107

Chapter 11: Putting Your First Interview Experience
to Good Use 118

References.. 129
Appendix... 135

Appreciation is extended to Laura Donatelli for
her assistance with editing this text.

To order copies of this book contact Nancy Maynes at
nancym@nipissingu.ca or visit our book website at
http://tenthingsinterviews.weebly.com/index.html

NOTES

CHAPTER 1

INTRODUCTION/CONTEXT

Interviews and Other Torturous Experiences

As you work your way through this book, you will see that we have tried to create a handbook that blends the reality of landing that first teaching job, with the paradox of trying to capture the attention of those who do the hiring in a brief interview format, with a bit of humor generated from our personal experiences in being interviewed and in interviewing others.

There is nothing quite so disconcerting as an interview. It is by its purpose a judgmental situation. That creates anxiety for the person being interviewed. The purpose of this book is to give you, the aspiring teacher, an inside view of the interview process from the perspective of the interviewer, with the purpose of helping to reduce your anxiety and replace it with solid and informed preparation.

"The Best Interview You Will Ever Have is the One You'll Have in the Car on the Way Home"

After people are interviewed for any type of job, their tendency is to leave the interview thinking, "I should have said . . .", as they reflect on how the interview went. Nervousness gets in the way of clear cognition during an interview and causes each of us to forget good points we might have used to illustrate an idea and to present our skills in the best possible way. Through strong preparation, including getting into the mindset of the interviewer as you prepare for a teaching interview, you can ensure that you maximize the brief interview time you have and optimize the impression you leave with the interviewers. This will make that drive home much more comfortable too!

Getting an Interview Invitation

Newly certified teachers know that the market for new teachers across Canada is very competitive. Several factors outside of your control will have an influence on the availability of jobs in teaching. These include: fewer students in the schools because the population is generally producing fewer school-aged children, changes in government policies, funding changes for education, fewer retirements among career teachers, and changes in mandatory retirement requirements in some jurisdictions. It has become almost expected that newly certified teachers will spend the first years of their career doing supply teacher work or vying for the coveted long-term contracts that will place them in one school for a period of time. Many jurisdictions expect new teachers to work their way up the chain of experience through supply teaching, to long term contracts, and finally to a permanent contract. Knowing this, the new teacher needs to be prepared for the interview to get onto the supply list for their jurisdiction and needs to be just as well prepared for this as if they were being interviewed for a full time permanent contract.

Hold On: The Only Thing that Ever Remains the Same Is That Everything Changes

While the teaching job market in Canada can be daunting for newly certified teachers as they start to search for jobs, there is hope for change on the horizon. Researchers anticipate a gradual increase in student population in about 2016 and for this trend to continue on the rise until about 2022 (Dedyna, 2011). This will be further affected by waves of retirement from longer-term teachers. This is a cycle of "boom and bust" that is not unusual in Canada. You just need to position yourself to be ready for the increased need for teachers when it happens. Brushing up on your interview skills will help you to be ready when the opportunities are open to you.

In 2011, two thirds of new teachers could not find full time employment in their teaching field (Dehaas, 2011). But, that means that one third of newly certified teachers **could** find full time employment. This book is about helping you to prepare to be part of the one third of fully employed teachers as soon as possible.

Statistics Canada provides information about teaching jobs, numbers of students in each province or territory, and hiring statistics. This information can provide you with current data about growth areas in this profession across the country and that may help with your planning. Stats Canada operates an Inquiry Line at 1-800-263-1136. As well, statistics are available online at http: www.statcan.gc.ca/pub/81-595-m/81-595-m2011095-eng.pdf. This link will lead you to government reports such as "Summary Public School Indicators for Canada, the Provinces and Territories, 2005/2006 to 2009/2010". Data on this site is provided as tables and graphs, which make comparisons of trends very easy.

Summary Public School Indicators for Canada, the Provinces and Territories, 2005/2006 to 2009/2010

Table A.12.1

Educators headcount in public elementary and secondary schools, Canada, provinces and territories, 2005/2006 to 2009/2010[1]

	Canada	N.L.	P.E.I.[2]	N.S.	N.B.	Que.	Ont.	Man.	Sask.[2,3]	Alta.[3]	B.C.	Y.T.	N.W.T.	Nvt.
							number							
2005/2006 Public	362,674	7,319	1,541	9,708	7,510	93,272	137,889	14,210	12,170	40,293	36,886	496	668 [e]	712
2006/2007 Public	378,621	7,402	1,547	9,919	7,629	96,130	149,713	14,248	12,445	40,556	37,149	510	671 [e]	702
2007/2008 Public	384,316	7,485	1,581	9,973	7,899	96,221	154,963	14,347	12,251	40,542	37,118	517	715 [e]	704
2008/2009 Public	388,808	7,542	1,638	10,064	8,077	96,098	157,303	14,321	12,406	42,515	36,921	550	720 [e]	653
2009/2010 Public	393,494	7,722	1,646	10,174 [p]	7,998	96,928	158,173	14,333	12,597	45,624	36,372	570	706	651

[e]   estimate
[p]   preliminary
1.   Care should be taken with cross jurisdictional comparison. The proportion of educators (comprising a mix of teachers, administrators and pedagogical support) and their respective remuneration, differs in each jurisdiction.
2.   Educational Assistants are not included.
3.   All educators in Lloydminster are included in Saskatchewan's counts and none of them are captured in the counts for Alberta.

Connect to other information about teaching jobs in Canada through http://www.statcan.gc.ca/pub/81-595-m/81-595-m2011095-eng.pdf.

Also, by using an online search engine to search "Canadian Statistics on Teacher Hiring", new graduates are able to get current information about trends and possibilities in the countrywide teacher job market.

Information related to teaching markets is often available from media sources. For example, the June 15, 2011 edition of *MacLean's* magazine provided statistics about the percentages of teacher graduates who got permanent jobs in their field in the first year after graduation. This is information that can help you develop a realistic view of marketplace conditions in teaching as these evolve.

The World is a Big Place

A quick reminder about job mobility might be wise here. On July I, 1995, the First Ministers of Canada signed the Agreement on International Trade (AIT). This agreement was designed to eliminate barriers to labour mobility as well as the movement of persons, goods, services, and investments across the country. In specific reference to teachers and their mobility across Canada, the First Ministers agreed in principle:

> . . . to reduce barriers to teacher mobility. It is intended to allow any teacher who holds a teaching credential in one province or territory to have access to teacher certification in any other province or territory in order to be eligible for employment opportunities in the teaching profession. (Council of Ministers of Education, n.d.)

In recent times, some provinces, such as Saskatchewan, are hiring teachers from other jurisdictions in promising numbers. If you are able to relocate, you should look into such opportunities to secure your first full-time contract in teaching. Additionally, Canadian certified teachers are well regarded around the world as being among the best-prepared professionals. Consider a world adventure for a year or two to get further experience in your field. Sites such as *www.joyjobs.com* will help you get started to see what opportunities may be available in teaching in an international context.

CHAPTER 2

KNOW THE PROCESS: APPLYING FOR A TEACHING POSITION

Timing Is Everything!

When applying for that important first teaching position, timing is crucial. If you want to teach for a particular school board, in a particular community, and even in a particular school, you have got to stay well informed about the openings. In recent years this often involves checking the board's web site regularly since positions will be posted electronically at the same time they are posted internally in a board. If you get into the habit of checking the web site daily, you'll be sure to be on top of the opportunities and in tune with the timelines.

Internal and External Postings

A school board's first allegiance is to the group of teachers already under its employ. In many jurisdictions, the school board has a working agreement with its teachers' federations that gives the already employed teachers the first opportunity to apply for any upcoming jobs with the board. In some jurisdictions, if only one teacher applies for an internal advertisement (often referred to as a posting), no interviews are held and the job goes immediately to the internal applicant. In this way, the federation has worked with employers to serve the best interests of the teachers. These postings for teaching jobs are called *internal postings*.

Internal postings can create a domino effect within a board as new jobs are sought and obtained and teachers begin to move from one school to another. However, the internal posting process can also take up a considerable amount of time as teachers who are already employed by the board move to new positions, and the positions they leave become available and must be filled by either an internal or an external posting.

External postings are advertisements for those jobs that cannot be filled by a teacher already employed by the school Board and must therefore be advertised to non-employed, certified teachers.

When you apply in response to an external posting, be very careful about meeting the timelines identified in the posting. Typically, boards cannot be flexible about these timelines so a posting that says, "Midnight, August 1st" means exactly that. An application that is received late even by one minute will usually be refused by the board. This practice creates an even playing field and helps the board avoid complaints about unfair process. Remember, in teaching, "on time" always means early!

Many jurisdictions subscribe to a website recruitment service called *Apply to Teach*. This service is available online at *www. applytoeducation.com/*. Some jurisdictions have their own site related to recruitment of teachers but increasingly searches for application processes to a specific school board will direct applicants to the *Apply to Teach* website. You need to be aware of how the boards, which most interest you, go about filling their teacher openings. Some sites also provide direction for teacher applicants about what documents they will need to provide when they apply for a position.

If you are interested in teaching positions outside of Canada, *Apply to Teach* has an "Education Global" tab that will direct you to a wide range of options. You can also access these options by phone at 1-877-900-5627.

Unsolicited Applications

Most Boards of Education do not accept unsolicited applications for teaching positions. Rather, they post positions as they open. Interested teachers are then directed when, where, and how to apply. If you take an unsolicited resume or application to a school or a board office, it will most likely be discarded. Instead, spend that valuable time polishing your resume and checking sites of interest to ensure that you apply for new postings as soon as they come up on the site.

Supporting Documentation

Usually, the posted job opening will also identify a specific set of documents that are required along with your application. Be sure your entire package is complete before you send in the application. Where applications are being received electronically, you usually will not be able to complete your application unless every required document has been downloaded. Where applications are to be handed in by hard copy, it will leave the best impression if the whole package is complete and easy to navigate so that reviewers can find all of the required pieces at a glance. The requirements of an application often include evidence of your certification, a recent vulnerable sector criminal reference check, and evidence of your membership or standing in the local governing body for teachers (e.g., Ontario College of Teachers, Teacher Regulation Branch of the B.C. Ministry of Education, etc.). Some jurisdictions may also use an online submission process that allows you to add supporting documentation to your application. For example, the B.C. Ministry of Education uses Makeafuture.ca, where applicants can insert professional e-portfolios into their application and track job opportunities through Facebook and Twitter links.

Some boards, especially larger ones, require that supporting documents, such as portfolios, be submitted electronically, while others will prefer and accept hard copies. Know what the requirements are for the jurisdictions that interest you and follow those guidelines. The more complete and compliant your package is when you apply, the better represented you are to the team of decision makers who receive your application. So, read the call for applications very carefully then make a list of what is required in documentation and another list of what is optional. Include as many of the optional documents as possible given the time limits for the posting. More information is usually better than not enough, but ease of access is crucial to both required and optional documents. A good professional practice is to keep your documents updated on a weekly basis so that you can be ready to apply as opportunities arise.

A Word About Quality

In a competitive job market, it is critical that every professional document you produce represents you in the best possible way. Professional documents need to have a polished look, be concise and to the point, and communicate clearly and accurately. Correct grammar will help to ensure that your application makes it past human resources screening and gets into the hands of school-based hiring teams.

It is, therefore, not enough to complete an application. You must complete it well and treat the entire application process with the highest esteem. People who view your application will resent lost time if your documents are untidy, disorganized, or contain grammar mistakes. It is worth the effort to have someone proofread every document before you include it in an application. Even if your grammar is very strong, just working with the same documents over and over causes you to start skimming when you check, and that can lead to errors being overlooked. Work hard to ensure that what you submit for employment represents you in the best professional light.

CHAPTER 3

GET YOUR PAPER WORK IN ORDER TO HELP YOU STAND OUT: YOUR RESUME AND SUPPORTING DOCUMENTATION

In the previous chapter, some ideas about completing the application process online were mentioned. This included some reference to the quality of the documents you submit with your application. In this chapter, some guidance about preparing those documents and structuring them to support your application will be provided.

There are two types of documents that are usually required as part of a teaching application. These include:

1. Factual records - including your resume, vulnerable sector criminal reference check, certification documents, transcripts, additional qualification records, etc.

2. Evidence records - including samples of documents that demonstrate your professional skills (e.g., a classroom management plan, lesson plans, unit plans, assignments you have designed, letters of reference, practicum evaluations, etc.).

Boards will be very clear about which factual record documents are required to accompany your teaching application and which evidence records they want to see. Many jurisdictions provide a checklist or an access gate on a web site that will guide your inclusion of these documents. Some Boards may make the inclusion of evidentiary documents (e.g., a portfolio or an e-portfolio) optional. If evidentiary documents are optional and you are granted a teaching interview, be sure to bring them to the interview. Later chapters will address how you should use these pieces of evidence during the interview to your best advantage.

Many Faculty of Education programs will require that you develop a professional portfolio as part of your program. They may also provide guidance about how to develop an e-portfolio. It is fairly common practice for larger school boards to accept only an e-portfolio as an application document so you must have this ready well ahead of predictable timelines.

If you have not had instruction in how to prepare a teaching portfolio during your teacher preparation, there are some excellent online sources that can provide sound guidance. The site at *http://www.wikihow.com/Create-a-Teacher-Portfolio* is an example of a well-organized and informative site that will provide step-by-step directions and provide links to software to help you with your e-portfolio.

Other online sources that you may find useful as you develop your portfolio include:

> *http://www.fctl.ucf.edu/FacultySuccess/ ProfessionalPortfolios/content/portfolioinclude.pdf*
>
> *http://www2.scholastic.com/browse/article.jsp?id=4148*
>
> *http://www.duq.edu/cte/academic-careers/ teaching-portfolio.cfm*
>
> *http://www.cs.tufts.edu/~ablumer/portfolio.html#What*

Your Teaching Resume

Often, newly certified teachers are facing the task of producing their first professional resume as they apply for their first teaching position. This is a task that requires a great deal of time and attention to detail to create an effective resume. However, the time and attention you give this will pay off. This is the single most influential document in helping to secure you an interview. If you can't get an interview, you have no opportunity to show people how perfect you are for this job!

You want to ensure you have a resume that does two things effectively. It needs to summarize your accomplishments succinctly and thoroughly, while presenting your personality and individuality in ways that will get the document noticed. This is often a finely balanced task. Achieving an effective summary can be done through your choice of words and format, including finely crafted section headings. Presenting your personality and individuality in ways that will draw attention can be achieved by attending to colour, artistic layout, and graphic design elements that have professional appeal. Resumes can go badly wrong if you don't strike the right balance between these two purposes. Some examples of how to achieve this balance are provided in the next few pages.

The first example contains a sample of a cover letter. Cover letters may be required as part of your application but this can vary by board. A cover letter should identify the position you are applying for, comment on your skills and suitability for the position, and identify the items you have included in your application package.

Example 1

YOUR NAME

Your Street • City, Ontario Postal Code • Cellular: (Area Code)-xxx.xxxx
your name@hotmail.com
Ontario College of Teachers #XXXXXX

Monday February 11, 20XX

Name, Principal
Fellowes High School
420 Bell Street
Pembroke, ON, K8A 2K5

Dear Name:

Please accept this cover letter and résumé as my official application for a position as a Non-Credit Literacy Instructor at Fellowes High School as posted on the Jobs in Education website (file number **SEC 2790**). Since attaining my Bachelor of Education degree in the Concurrent Education program at Nipissing University, I am eager to begin my career as a teacher. I am qualified to teach Primary, Junior, Intermediate, and Senior English divisions; as well I have Special Education Part 1 credentials. Furthermore, I plan to obtain Reading Part 1 additional qualifications this spring.

Over the past five years I have acquired a total of twenty-three weeks of in-class practicum experience in a variety of schools and classrooms, which have enabled me to grow and flourish as a teacher. During this time I have had the opportunity to teach in multiple schools in the Renfrew County District School Board, as well as a Section 23 classroom, and an international classroom in Kenya, Africa. My strengths as outlined in my practice teaching reports include a strong commitment to student learning, the ability to encourage pupil participation and responsibility, the creation of detailed lesson plans, and effective classroom management skills. Moreover, I have dedicated much of my time helping others in areas of Language and Literacy by volunteering at Nipissing University's Writing Drop-In Centre, Peer Mentoring program, and most recently at the local Kumon tutoring organization.

My primary belief about education is that all students have the capacity to learn, and my primary goal as an educator is academic and personal success for all students. I am strongly interested in working as a Non-Credit Literacy Instructor, as I have much to offer in terms of commitment, drive, and enthusiasm for the teaching profession, and Language and Literacy in particular. Given my related experience, capabilities and enthusiasm for teaching and learning I am confident that I will be an asset to your school. You will find my resume attached; please feel welcome to contact me if you need further information. Thank you for your consideration, and I look forward to hearing from you.

Sincerely,

Your Name
B.Ed. (Concurrent), B.A. Honours (English)

YOUR NAME

Your Street • City, Ontario Postal Code • Cellular: (Area Code)-XXX-XXXX
your name@hotmail.com
Ontario College of Teachers #XXXXXX

EDUCATION

December 2012	**EDUCATION IN THE SENIOR DIVISION- ENGLISH** Nipissing University, North Bay, Ontario
June 2012	**SPECIAL EDUCATION PART ONE** Nipissing University, North Bay, Ontario
May 2012	**EDUCATION IN THE PRIMARY DIVISION** Nipissing University, North Bay, Ontario
June 2012	**BACHELOR OF EDUCATION** Nipissing University Schulich Faculty of Education, North Bay, Ontario Concurrent Education program, Junior/Intermediate Divisions English Teachable iTeach Laptop Learning Program

June 2012	**BACHELOR OF ARTS**
	Nipissing University, North Bay, Ontario
	English (Honours) Major, with Distinction

June 2007	Fellowes High School, Renfrew, Ontario
	Graduated with honours and a gold certificate in French

Scholarships:
2007 - 2010	Carl Sanders Scholarship, Nipissing University
2010	Dr. Herbert A. Bruce Chapter IODE Julie Hewitt Memorial Scholarship, Nipissing University

Accomplishments
2011	Presented in the annual English Studies Student Symposium, Nipissing University
2011	Presented in the annual Undergraduate Research Conference, Nipissing University

Professional Development
2011	Tribes Training
2011	North-eastern Ontario Regional Arts Conference (NORAC)
2010	Imagination and Creativity Education (ICE) Conference
2010	Pass the Play Workshop- Literacy games for elementary schools

Volunteer Experience
2012	Kumon Math and Reading Aid, North Bay, Ontario
2010	Writing Drop-In Centre Assistant, Nipissing University

Career Related Experience
February 2013	ELEMENTARY OCCASIONAL TEACHER
	XXXXXX County District School Board—Waiting list

November 2012	**CASUAL/SUPPLY EDUCATIONAL ASSISTANT**
	Renfrew County District School Board

- Ability and knowledge of working with children with special education needs
- Worked collaboratively with all members of the assigned schools
- Implemented daily programs as directed by absent Educational Assistants

July-August 2012   **SUPPORT WORKER**

Southside Community Centre, Petawawa, Ontario
- Worked one-on-one and shared support with children with special needs
- Implemented a variety of strategies directed towards the goal of inclusion
- Communicated daily with counsellors and parents to ensure that the child's needs were being effectively supported

March-April 2012   **GRADE SEVEN PRE-SERVICE TEACHER**

Herman Street Public School, Petawawa, Ontario
- Planned, implemented, and analyzed differentiated Mathematics, Language, History, Physical Education, and Health lessons 100% of the day
- Ensured that IEP accommodations and modifications were regularly met
- Developed and used assessment devices (rubrics, checklists, anecdotal records)

February 2012   **INTERNATIONAL PRE-SERVICE TEACHER**

Emori Joi School, Kenya, Africa
- Taught a grade seven class of 54 English as a Second Language students
- Prepared and implemented daily Language, Social Studies, Mathematics, Physical Education, and Creative Arts lessons with minimal resources
- Focused on classroom management, problem solving, and decision making skills

January 2012   **PRE-SERVICE TEACHER IN A SECTION 23 CLASS**

New Horizons, St. Thomas the Apostle School, Renfrew, Ontario
- Partook in anxiety group counselling sessions with at-risk adolescents and the classroom therapist
- Attended IPRC meetings for students in transition
- Planned differentiated lessons tailored to each student's high school courses

Spring 2010/2011 **GRADE SIX TUTOR IN THE CLASSROOM**

Our Lady of Sorrows Catholic School, Petawawa, Ontario

Herman Street Public School, Petawawa, Ontario

- Helped students prepare for the EQAO standardized test
- Assisted students both individually and in small groups with specified Mathematics and Language skills
- Prepared daily lessons that focused on each student's area(s) of need
- Scribed for students as directed by their Individual Education Plans

YOUR NAME

Your Street • City, Ontario Postal Code • Cellular: (Area Code)-XXX-XXXX

your name @hotmail.com

Ontario College of Teachers' #XXXXXX

REFERENCES

Referee Name

International Practicum Supervisor

705-474-3461 (ext. XXXX)

XXXXXXX@nipissingu.ca

Referee Name

Associate Teacher

Herman Street Public School Teacher

613-XXX-XXXX

XXXXX@sympatico.ca

Referee Name

International Practicum Supervisor

Nipissing University

Schulich School of Education

(705)-474-3461 (ext. XXXX)

XXXX@nipissingu.ca

Referee Name
Associate Teacher
New Horizons, Day Treatment Program for Adolescents
(613)- XXX-XXXX
XXXXX@dsbn.com
I, YOUR NAME, grant permission for my references to be contacted.

This sample cover letter and resume should provide some guidance for you as you prepare your application package. Two additional resume samples follow. Compare these to determine the styles you prefer and decide how you would like to present your resume.

Example 2

YOUR NAME

12 Your Street Drive
Your City, ON Canada XXX XXX
(705) XXX - XXXX
XXXXXXXX@nipissingu.ca

WORK EXPERIENCE

Instructional Designer   Nipissing University
Bracebridge, Ontario   September 2010 - Present

- Designed courses for the online environment for the Faculty of Arts and Science, the Faculty of Applied and Professional Schools, and the Schulich School of Education
- Developed and presented professional development sessions for faculty on relevant teaching topics (such as teaching in the digital age)
- Co-created and developed the Mobile Experiential Leadership Development program (MELD), which enabled high school students to earn dual credits for a Senior Social Sciences course, and a first year University Success course, in a two-week residential program

iTeach Educational Instructor   Nipissing University
North Bay, Ontario   September 2003 - September 2010

- Provided educational technology and instructional support, and development for faculty and students
- Organized and implemented annual educational technology conferences, for students and faculty enrolled in the BEd program
- Developed and organized workshops and training sessions for faculty and students
- Supervised 25+ Student Technology Assistant employees to provide in-class support, drop-in centres and education software workshops for faculty and students
- Developed and maintained a student educational support resource for faculty and students
- Nominated for Part-Time Teaching Award 2007 and 2010

Science and Technology Transfer Intern   Canadian Ecology Centre
Mattawa, Ontario .   May 2003 - September 2003
- Instructed outdoor education programs in Geographic Information Systems, ecology, GPS, forestry, wetlands, canoeing, digital cameras and drumming
- Assisted with technology transfer initiatives for the Forestry Research Partnership, such as event planning (workshops, seminars, and tours) and maintenance of the extensive product library and catalogue
- Assisted with computer-related troubleshooting, technology updates, and website development and maintenance

Ontario's Living Legacy Resource Manager   Ministry of Natural
                                                         Resources
Red Lake, Ontario   April 2001 - January 2002
- Designed and implemented a program on Sustainable Development for grade seven students

Supply Teacher   District School Board Ontario Northeast
Cochrane, Ontario   October 2000 - March 2001
- Assisted students with assignments and answered questions concerning schoolwork, while managing and motivating students to promote self-confidence and productivity

EDUCATION

Master of Education
Nipissing University, North Bay, Ontario   May 2004-April 2010

Bachelor of Education, Junior/Intermediate Division
Primary Additional Basic Qualification
Nipissing University, North Bay, Ontario   September 2002-June 2003

Bachelor of Environmental Studies, Specialized Honours
Certificate in Geographic Information Systems and Remote Sensing
York University, North York, Ontario   September 1996-June 2001

RESEARCH AND PUBLICATIONS

Master's of Education Thesis   Nipissing University, April 2010
Thesis: *Student Teacher Motivation and Technology Learning Opportunities*
Bachelor of Environmental Studies Undergraduate Thesis
                                             York University, June 2001
Thesis: *Space Debris Re-entry as a Preventative Measure: Hazards and Benefits of Intentional De-Orbiting of Debris in the Near-Earth Atmosphere*

VOLUNTEER EXPERIENCE

Big Sisters of Nipissing   North Bay, Ontario
- **Website Maintenance** assisting with the development and the ongoing maintenance of the Big Sisters of Nipissing website

Founders College, York University Toronto, Ontario
- **Peer Tutor** offering general academic assistance for students attending the college. I assisted students with writing and editing reports.

Big Sisters of York Region Aurora, Ontario
- **Big Sister** responsible for a young teenager, working on a one-to-one basis in the interest of providing guidance and positive values

REFERENCES

Dr. XXXX   Dr. XXXX
Associate Professor,   Associate Dean of Education,
Nipissing University   Nipissing University
705-474-3450 ext XXXX   705-474-3450 ext XXXX

Dr. XXXX   Mr. XXXX
Assistant Professor,   Assistant Professor,
Nipissing University   Nipissing University
705-474-3450 ext XXXX   705-474-3450 ext XXXX

Additional References Available Upon Request

When you look at resume examples, consider the following questions:

- What does this resume do very well?
- Does its format fit how you want your resume to be presented?
- Does this sample present all of the required information?
- Would you change the order of presentation of any information?
- Are there things you would like to do differently on your resume? Why?

If you look at sample resumes critically with an eye to what you find impressive about each one, you will be close to examining them in the same way that prospective employers would.

Example 3

Your Name

Your address, Strathmore, City, Postal Code
Work: xxx-xxx-xxxx   Cell: xxx-xxx-xxxx
Email: xxxxxxxxxx@mac.com

Ontario College of Teachers' Registration #XXXXXX
Alberta Education Certificate #XXXXXXN

Profile

I am a highly motivated, technologically adept teaching professional. In my classroom, students can expect an integrated and collaborative learning experience built on a philosophy of constructivism. I believe that every student can learn and that there are no bad students, just inhibiting behaviours. In a faculty environment, I bring a wealth of technological knowledge and experience in training adults in the use of digital learning tools. I am a strong problem solver, a creative thinker, and I am able to collaborate as part of a team.

Education

- Nipissing University, North Bay, Ontario - Bachelor of Education - May 2012
  - Primary, Junior, and Intermediate (English) Divisions
  - Kindergarten Theory & Practice Option Course
  - iTeach Laptop Learning Program
  - Overall A+ course average
- University of Guelph, Guelph, Ontario - Honours Bachelor of Arts - February 2008
  - English & History Double Major

Additional Qualifications

- Nipissing University, North Bay, Ontario
  - Teaching Students with Communication Needs (Autism Spectrum Disorders) - August 2012
  - English as a Second Language, Part 1 - August 2012
  - Special Education, Part 1 - August 2012

Teaching Experience

Central Bow Valley School - Grades 5, 6, 7, & 8
Gleichen, Alberta, Golden Hills School Division #75   **2012-2013**
  - taught two combined classes (5/6 & 7/8) on a full-time, permanent contract
  - differentiated for 15 fully-integrated students coded as exceptional according to Alberta Learning guidelines, and 46 students with documented past or ongoing trauma
  - responsible for instruction in language arts, social studies, outdoor ed, design and technology, and art
  - developed and implemented lessons, and assessed student learning according to the Alberta Curriculum and the Prioritized Curriculum as outlined by the school division
  - volunteered for extra-curricular clubs during recess and after school
  - participated in weekly school-wide planning meetings and collaborative evaluations
  - developed and implemented several new technology plans school-wide, including the use of iPads, ActivBoards, Smart TVs (AppleTV), and collaborative software (Evernote, Moodle, & Mahara).

Practice Teaching Experience

Howard Robertson Public School - Grade 3
Kitchener, Ontario, Waterloo Regional District School Board   **2012**
  - taught 100% of class time for 1 week, 75% for 1 week, and 50% for 4 weeks during a 6-week practicum

Your Name

- worked with 21 students, including 8 students who were first-generation immigrants and ESL learners, 3 students who had IEPs for behavioural challenges, and 2 students who had IEPs for reading
- developed, implemented, and assessed units on 3-digit addition and subtraction and probability for the grade 3 curriculum, while utilizing the 3-Part Lesson Plan and providing opportunities for inquiry-based learning
- developed, implemented, and assessed an integrated Social Studies, Language, and Visual Arts unit over a 6-week period, culminating in a diorama project which compared the Early Settlement period in Upper Canada to modern life
- co-taught a gym unit in Basketball, and began a unit in Soccer
- developed 35 lessons which utilized SMARTBoard technology as part of regular instruction
- was assessed and coached by a Waterloo Board Mathematics Consultant
- participated in EQAO planning meetings and implemented strategies as part of regular mathematics and literacy instruction
- participated in weekly grade-wide and division-wide planning meetings, and collaboratively evaluated student work with 3 other grade 3 teachers
- volunteered for extra-curricular clubs during recess and after school

Floradale Public School - Grade 4/5 Combined
Floradale, Ontario, Waterloo Regional District School Board   **2011**
- taught 100% of class time for 3 weeks, 75% for 1 week, and 50% for 2 weeks during a 6-week practicum
- worked with 29 students, including 20 students who were ESL learners, 2 students with autism, and 2 students with physical challenges (1 for hearing and 1 for mobility)
- was responsible for all instruction in Science, Social Studies, Music, Health, and Physical Education, and was partially responsible for instruction in Visual Arts, Mathematics, and Language
- developed, implemented, and assessed a unit of explanatory writing, while integrating Visual Arts and Music with the Language curriculum
- developed, implemented, and assessed a Social Studies culminating research project, which integrated the use of collaborative software (Evernote) to facilitate students working together to create poster and present a comparison of a Medieval occupation to its modern equivalent
- taught components of the Geometry and Spatial Sense, as well as the Number Sense strands for the grade 4 Mathematics curriculum
- co-taught a gym unit in Volleyball, and taught a unit on Dance and Movement
- participated in division-wide CASI planning and review meetings

Career Experience
Foreign English Teacher, Global Education Center, Woonjin Think Big
Wondang-dong, Seo-gu, Incheon, South Korea   **2009-2010**
- taught English at a private academy to school-aged children between ages 4 and 16
- designed lessons, games, and worksheets for 16 curriculum levels, from basic phonetics to university-level English literature
- wrote 3 original course manuals, including lesson plans, keynote presentations, crafts, and activities for 12-week semester programs that are still currently being taught at the Global Education Center
- created 73 Adobe Flash-based computer games, based on the Global Education Center curriculum

Your Name

Individual Training Specialist, Equitable Life Insurance Company of Canada
Waterloo, Ontario   2007-2009
- responsible for assessing the gaps in knowledge of a division with over 400 employees
- researched and wrote technical manuals on systems, procedures, and products
- presented on a diverse range of topic to groups of up to 120 participants
- provided accurate timelines and cost estimates of proposed training for manager evaluation
- provided ongoing feedback to managers as to the effectiveness of training
- gained an expert understanding of all industry-standard products, computer systems, and software
- designed and launched a web-based help system containing over 1100 reference articles

Volunteer Experience
Guest Speaker - "Meeting the Needs of Exceptional Learners"
Calgary Board of Education, Calgary, Alberta   2013
- presented a classroom management system designed to support the learning of students with exceptionalities and trauma to an audience of teachers, teaching assistants, and administrators

Student Technology Assistant
Nipissing University, North Bay, Ontario   2011-2012
- volunteered weekly to staff a technological assistance drop-in centre for the university community
- provided daily technical support to peers and faculty during lectures and seminars
- assisted with SMARTBoards, tablets, Mac and PC laptops, data projectors, response systems, and productivity software

Adult Volunteer, Elementary School Education Assistance
North Bay, Ontario   2012
- worked with children ages 4 and 5 in a full-day Kindergarten class in the Near North District School Board
- focused primarily on language and math skills while practising scaffolded questioning and observation techniques
- developed interactive digital tools and assets based on best teaching practices for a newly installed SMARTBoard for the use of the regular classroom teacher

Elmira and Floradale, Ontario   2009
- worked with children between ages 4 and 14 in 2 Ontario public schools in the Waterloo Region District School Board
- focused primarily on language, literacy, and math skills, spending a total of 459 hours volunteering
- worked with students of varied backgrounds: 2 students had behavioural issues, 5 students had high-functioning autism, 3 were gifted, and 18 were English as a second language learners

Your Name

Leader, CISV International Interchange
Waterloo, Ontario   **2009**
- worked with 8 youths aged 12-14 to undertake a month-long cultural exchange with 8 youths from Norway
- conducted a program designed by CISV International to foster global peace by having youths develop global friendships and accept cultural diversity
- was the sole adult legally responsible for 8 youths for a full 5 weeks, 3 of which were abroad

Certifications & Professional Development
Digital Citizenship Committee
Strathmore, Alberta   **2012-2013**
- collaborated with teachers, instructional coaches, and administrators to help create a digital citizenship policy document and guidelines for staff and students in Golden Hills School Division #75

Junior High Inquiry Learning Community
Strathmore, Alberta   **2012-2013**
- collaborated with teachers and instructional coaches to plan and implement inquiry learning and meaningful tasks into daily social studies work

Digital Learning Tools Projects I, II, & III
Strathmore, Alberta   **2012-2013**
- collaborated with teachers and instructional coaches from across the school division to integrate WordQ, SpeakQ and iPad technologies into classrooms.
- participated in goal setting, assessment, and data collection to inform Golden Hills School Division's technology planning

Nipissing University Workshops
North Bay, Ontario   **2011-2012**
- iTools for iOS Training Session
- Digital Cameras Training Session
- Digital Storytelling Training Session
- Digital Photography Software Training Session
- ePublications Training Session
- Creating Educational Games Training Session
- Learn360 Training Session
- SMARTBoards Training Session
- SMART Notebook 1 Training Session
- SMART Notebook 2 Training Session
- Claymation Training Session
- Classroom Comics Training Session
- Adaptive/Assistive Technology Training Session
- Response Systems Training Session

Your Name

- Web 2.0 Training Session
- Blogging for Educators Training Session
- Blended Learning Training Session
- "Why is my Blackberry sitting on a pile of books?" a seminar by Dr. David Booth
- "AODA and the Accessibility Standards for Customer Service in Educational Settings" a workshop by the Government of Ontario

Beyond Consequences Institute
Online (Strathmore, Alberta)   2013
- certified as having completed the "Help for Billy" Trauma Intervention Training Course

Crisis Prevention Institute (CPI)
North Bay, Ontario   2012
- certified as having completed the Nonviolent Crisis Intervention Training Course

TRIBES Learning Community
North Bay, Ontario   2011
- certified as having completed the Tribes TLC Basic Course

Conferences
Calgary, Alberta   2013
- Palliser District Teachers' Convention
Calgary, Alberta   2012
- Using and Assessing Student Responses to Open Questions in Grades 3-6 Math with Marion Small-Calgary Regional Consortium
North Bay, Ontario   2012
- Multimodality and Multiliteracies: Rethinking Literacy Learning for Contemporary Classrooms
North Bay, Ontario   2011
- Northeastern Ontario Regional Arts Conference (NORAC)
- Imagination, Creativity, Education (ICE)

Awards
- J.W. Trusler Proficiency Award - Education - received June 2012
- Elementary Teachers' Federation of Ontario Award - received June 2012
- Elementary Teachers' Federation of Ontario Faculty of Education Award - received June 2012
- Primary-Junior Division iTeach Integration Award - received June 2012
- Phyllis Leleu Kitchen Award for Creative Writing - received June 2003

Be Professionally Analytical

Look closely at these three examples of teachers' resumes. Does one appeal to you more than the other? Are you responding to the factual elements or the design elements or to the balance between the two? What would you do differently with each example?

Let's Try Building Your Professional Resume

Building a resume starts with a sorting exercise. First, decide which headings are relevant to the position you want. As you make these decisions, read Board and school web sites to see if key phrases give you ideas about what potential employers value and envision in their jurisdiction. Write each heading that you decide to use on a separate sheet of paper. Now, use post-it notes to brainstorm ideas you might want to add under each heading to reflect your experience and achievements in each area. As you write each note, sort it under the headings. Once the brainstorming is complete you can work through each heading pile and examine, adjust wording, discard, and put items into time order with the most recent at the top of each pile (i.e., reverse time order).

As you move on the next step of building your resume, you need to remind yourself that you are applying for a professional teaching position. While you may have years of valuable experience in another employment role, only the tasks that are transferrable to teaching are relevant in your new resume. So, be ruthless at this point. Cull out any experience that does not apply directly to teaching. Once your resume has been drafted you may want to re-insert some of the most recent and most closely related non-teaching employment or volunteer experiences you've had. Choose those that highlight either your values related to community endeavors or those that demonstrate your leadership skills. Every aspect of the final resume document should provide evidence of your abilities as they will relate to teaching skills.

Finally, put the first thing last. Design a professional letterhead that you will use on your application cover letter, your resume, and on selected documents in your professional portfolio. The letterhead should contain your full name as you want to be known professionally, your full address, phone contact information, and an email address.

Example

Marilyn E. Hanniford

12 Blackberry Lane
Rockville, B. C.
VOK 2R4
Phone: 604-925-9983 (cell)
marilynh@gmail.com

Here are a few words of caution about your letterhead. First, enlarge your name and use a professional looking script for it. This will make it stand out among a pile of other resumes. Be cautious if you plan to use colour. Be sure you select a tasteful colour that draws attention but is not too bold. Mixing colours for this purpose is not a good idea. Second, identify the type of phone number or numbers you are providing (e.g., cell, work, home). This allows users to select the most appropriate time to call you. Third, check the details you have provided very carefully. You don't want to miss a call about an interview because you typed a wrong digit in your phone number! Fourth (and a very important point!) be sure you provide a professionally selected and appropriate email address. An email address such as mhparty.ca is not likely to draw the type of attention you want in this context. Finally, if your contact information changes at any time during the application process, be sure to contact potential employers and provide updated information.

Can you do the job? Will you love the job? Will we love working with you?

Some employers say that there are really only three key questions that they need to know about those employees they seek to hire: **Can you do the job? Will you love the job?** and **Will we**

love working with you? Your resume is designed to address the first of these three questions.

Potential employers want to see that you have already amassed a body of evidence that displays your competence and commitment. Past experiences provide this evidence. How you display your past experiences in the best way is crucial. As you build your resume, expand on each key heading of your resume by starting each point with an active verb. Verbs such as "collected", "lead", "taught", "designed", and "implemented" are powerful in the impression they leave. They speak of your confidence and self-assurance, which will impress an employer and build their confidence in your ability to do the job.

The list below is a way to check each aspect of good resume building as you complete each part of this process.

Resume Building Checklist

- Visit Board web sites to help you decide on areas to highlight in your resume.
- Decide on sub-titles to use within your resume.
- Brainstorm key ideas to include under each sub-title.
- Sort key ideas under sub-titles.
- Discard irrelevant items.
- Organize experiences under each sub-title by reverse time order.
- Check each entry of key ideas to be sure each one starts with an active, past tense verb.
- Check each inclusion to be sure that it provides solid evidence of your skills and abilities as a teacher.
- Design your professional letterhead.
- Lay out the resume to achieve the final look you want.

One last but perhaps most critical piece of advice about your resume is important here. NEVER send out a resume without having at least one other person check it over for you very carefully. By the time you have completed your resume, you have been working on it for many hours. You need a second pair of eyes to check it for spelling and layout mistakes (e.g., inconsistent spacing, changes of verb tense, irrelevant information, etc.). It is often astonishing to see what things another person will see in your resume that you didn't notice after all your hard work.

A spelling mistake on a resume can be a disaster. The people who will consider your resume will have many to choose among and they will see a spelling mistake as an indication of professional carelessness.

Finally, be sure you are aware of resume requirements identified by the school jurisdictions that interest you. Some larger school boards limit resume length (e.g., 2 pages plus references). With online application systems, some software will only accept the first two pages of a resume. Be sure you are compliant with requirements. If you are not, your resume may never reach the people who will make hiring decisions.

Choosing and Identifying Your Referees

When you are applying for a teaching position, not all referees will be equally valuable to you. When potential employers get to the point of checking with your referees because they are considering offering you a job, the first question they will ask a referee is, "Have you seen him/her teach?" If the answer is, "No", that is the end of their questions. In teaching, your referees are used to provide testimony related to the second critical question that employers want to know . . . . **Can you do the job?**

It is, therefore very important that you list only referees who have seen you teach. Of course, the more frequently they have seen you teach, the better. Having seen you teach will allow your referees to be expansive with examples when specific questions are asked.

With your referees, there are several courtesies that you owe them if they are to act on your behalf by providing you with a reference. First, make sure you ask their permission to use them as a referee. When you ask, be specific about which job(s) you are applying for when this is happening. You do not want your referees to spend time on the phone if they are called expressing surprise about hearing from someone or trying to recall the times they worked with you. Also, be aware of what your referee will say about you. A little story will illustrate this point.

Years ago, as a Faculty Advisor who evaluated teacher candidates while they were engaged in practice teaching in schools, one of us worked with a young man who was struggling with his role as teacher. Through the months we worked together, I coached, advised, and monitored his work by examining his planning before he taught lessons. Even with considerable support, I had serious reservations about his suitability for the role of teacher. Later in the academic year, I learned that he had, without consent, listed me as a referee on his resume. If I had been called by a potential employer, I would not have been able to give a positive report of his abilities, and because I didn't know he had listed me as a reference, I might well have expressed surprise on the phone when speaking to the potential employer. You want to avoid both of these responses from your referees!

Also, in many situations, potential employers will not call all of your references. They are most likely to call the first two people on your referee list. So, be strategic. On your referee list, provide the names and contact information of the referees whom you know will be most effusive and positive about your skills and suitability for the job first, then list others who have agreed to be your referee but about whom you may be less certain.

You can also use some presentation strategies on your referee list that will work to your advantage. First, when you prepare the list, put your referees on a separate page from your resume proper. This will allow busy hiring committees to get support from other staff such as secretaries to call referees. Be sure you use your designed letterhead at the top of your referee list page. This will avoid the possibility that your list will get mixed up with someone else's. You could, alternatively, title that page "Referees for (Your Full Name)".

If you are applying for teaching positions over a number of years or changing positions within the system after a few years and still want to use a referee whom you may not have spoken to for some time, be sure to contact the person and ask if they will still provide you with a reference and explain what job you have in mind. This again will avoid a note of surprise in the referee's voice when he/she is called.

Finally, just a quick word about word usage. You may have noticed the words *referees* and *references* used in the paragraphs above. As you prepare your documents, be aware of the difference. A referee is a person, and they make a statement, or provide a reference for a candidate. Many people mix these up and refer to the people as their references. This is a fine distinction but in a climate where you are looking for every edge, you want to be aware of fine distinctions!

When you prepare your referee list, there are a few things you can do to make this list of referees stand out as part of your resume. First, fill the page. You can do this by making strategic choices about font size and spacing. Second, if you use a title for any referee (e.g., Mr., Ms., Mrs., Dr., Rev., etc.), apply a title to every one. Third, center the information about your referees on the page. This makes the page look fuller and the names more prominent. Finally, following each name, identify the person's role in relation to you (e.g., Associate Teacher, Faculty Supervisor, etc.).

Providing the correct and detailed information about your referees is important. You want to make contacting each person as easy and comfortable as possible for potential employers. To do this: provide as much contact information as you can (e.g., school name, phone numbers, email); identify each phone number by type (e.g., home, school, cell) to guide the employer about suitable calling times; provide the referee's first name so that the call can be casual in tone; if the referee's first name is androgynous (i.e., used for both females and males), add a title before all referee names.

A word about providing cell phone numbers on your resume is needed here. Cell phone use has caused us to become increasingly casual about how we respond to an incoming call. It is critical that you get into the habit of answering your cell phone in a professional way once you have provided that number as a contact on a resume or job application. Similarly, if you have provided a landline number and you share accommodation, which may mean that someone other than yourself may answer an incoming call, speak to those people about the importance of a professional response when they answer the phone and when they call you to the phone. This is all part of making that important first impression.

A sample referee page might look like this:

Referees for Marilyn E. Hanniford
12 Blackberry Lane
Rockville, B. C.
VOK 2R4
Phone: 604-925-9983 (cell)
marilynh@gmail.com

Mrs. Carol Chann
Associate Teacher, Wilding Public School
48 Wilding Court
Ajax, Ontario
L2P 3Z9
Phones: 416-926-4761 (school)
416-933-2431 (home)
416-526-2535 (cell)
Email: *carol.chann@hotmail.com*

Mr. Mark Dunn
Associate Teacher, Wildwoods Public School
567 Casswell Rd.
Ajax, Ontario
L4P 3O7
Phones: 416-926-5834 (school)
416-989-2831 (home)
416-526-8832 (cell)
Email: *mark.dunn@gmail.com*

Ms. Chantel Niche
Associate Teacher, Crossroads Elementary School
58 Corners Rd.
Ajax, Ontario
L5N 2P6
Phones: 416-926-5419 (school)
416-926-3888 (home)
416-538-2492 (cell)
Email: *chan.ni@hotmail.ca*

Dr. Fabian Roads
Faculty Advisor, Nipissing University
100 College Dr.
North Bay, Ontario
P1B 8L7
Phones: 705-474-3450 X925 (work)
705-840-5678 (home)
707-474-3891 (cell)
Email: dr. f. *roads@nipissingu.ca*

How Many Referees Do You Need?

How many referee contacts should you provide? Most school board web sites will ask you to identify three referees. However, you should always consider "going one better". If they ask for three, give them four. It is still critical, however, that every referee can say that they have seen you teach. Literally, callers' very next words will be, "Thank you for your time" if the referee says "No" to this initial question. When you are applying for a teaching position, only people who have seen you teach can serve as valuable referees. Also be aware that some boards may ask you to provide your referees and their contact information on a form they use for all applicants. If this is the case, there will be a link to such forms on the application web site. Be sure to use it if it is provided.

When you are preparing your resume and referee pages, as with any professional documents, it is well worth your time and effort to attend to small details. Note that the samples that are provided have attended to details of spacing, punctuation, font size, and consistency. These details will create the positive impression you need to get your application noticed.

If you build a strong resume that addresses the question "Can you do the job?" you have opened the door to getting the interview that will allow you to convince an employer that you will love the job and they will love working with you.

The Resume Cover Letter or Letter of Application

Most application processes require that you provide a cover letter as the initial document that accompanies your resume, your list of referees, and your professional portfolio. The cover letter does several things for you so it is important that you give its composition the time and attention it needs to create an impressive letter. This cover letter introduces you, establishes interest in what skills you have to offer, and situates your qualifications in relation to the posting for the job. See the sample cover letter that is provided in *Example 1* of this chapter.

Increasingly, potential employers scrutinize cover letters to determine the quality of an applicant's writing. Since the ability to communicate in written format is a critical skill for a teacher, this letter provides potential employers with their first opportunity to ensure that you have that skill.

Cover letters can feel awkward to write because you may feel like you've already said it all in your resume. Use this letter to provide some feeling for your personality to add a more individualized flavor to what it is in your resume.

When you chose what to write in this cover letter, be clear about the difference between providing your philosophy of education and briefly and concisely introducing your core beliefs by way of introducing yourself. You can do this by talking about what your classroom will be like instead of focusing on more general belief statements.

Cover letters, which might also be called applications letters, are typically brief. Try to make your letter one page long but no more. It makes a good first impression when you can get to the point succinctly and when your letterhead and signature appear on the same page.

A cover letter should be addressed to the person who is responsible for hiring for the posted position. If this person is not named in the posting, use a more general salutation such as "Dear Members of the Hiring Committee". Create an eye catching but professional looking letterhead that you use consistently on this letter, your resume, your referee list, and within your portfolio. This consistency will help employers see your attention to details and will present your qualifications as a package, which is impressive professionally. Be sure your letterhead contains the following details:

- your full name as you wish to be known professionally (it is wise to have this match your transcript information and other certification)
- your complete address, including postal code
- phone numbers, identified by type (i.e., home, work, cell)
- your email address (be sure it sounds professional; change it if it doesn't . . . this is not the time to show your sense of humor).

A sample letterhead was shown earlier in this chapter.

Other things that are addressed in a cover letter include:

- reference to the job you are applying for; many Boards use a reference number system for each posting and some postings tell applicants to cite the posting number when they apply; read the posting directions carefully and follow them closely;
- a brief explanation of your qualifications in relation to the job as posted;
- a brief, succinct outline of your beliefs about education; do not write this as a philosophy; rather it should explain what

your classroom will be like and why; this approach will help you write in a tone that supports your ownership of the approaches you describe; and

- a concise and direct closing statement; there is no need to include your phone number or email here because they are in your letterhead; use this closing to remind the reader of your enthusiasm and unique qualifications for the position.

As you write the cover letter, organize your thoughts into three well-connected paragraphs. The opening paragraph should reference the job posting and state your qualifications, including any that you will complete before the start date for the position. The second paragraph should be devoted to a description of your beliefs about education. Use assertive, action-oriented words in this paragraph to support the reader's confidence in your statements. Use words and phrases that reflect the uniqueness of the jurisdiction, as found in the local mission statement. Highlight unique qualifications you may have that relate to the local priorities (e.g., Tribes training). Close your letter with enthusiasm and energy. Your eagerness to take the posted job should be clear to the reader but be sure to maintain a professional tone. Enthuse, don't gush!

As you prepare this cover letter, keep in mind who will see it and how it will be used. It is highly unlikely to be read closely by people in the board's Human Resources Department as they receive your application package. However, it will be read closely by principals and teachers who will serve on a hiring team at the school level. These professionals are looking for someone who fits their beliefs about education, fits their job needs, and fits with their team. Remember the three key questions as you prepare this letter:

- *Can you do the job?* - Therefore you outline your qualifications.
- *Will you love the job?* - Therefore you show your "fit" for the job in terms of your beliefs and by showing an enthusiastic tone.
- *Will we love working with you?* - Therefore you show your personality, confidence, and commitment.

Once your cover letter is completed (a first draft!), check it word for word to ensure that you have avoided some common pitfalls. Check that you have avoided tentative phrases like, "I believe" or "I think". These slow down the flow of your letter, make you seem less sure of yourself, and take up valuable space you can use for more informative ideas. Be sure the tone is just right . . . confident but open to professional growth. Maintain a consistent font size and ensure that it's easily readable (e.g., 11 or 12 font).

Avoid language that is too personal, too casual, or slang. Similarly, avoid using philosophical statements or quotes from other sources, even well regarded educators. These will fit well as spacers in your portfolio but should be avoided in your cover letter. Finally, check your spelling very carefully, then check it again. In a competitive job market, even one spelling mistake can cause interviewers to relegate your application package to the "no" pile. It is always a good idea to have someone else look over your package specifically for spelling and grammar mistakes. Remember two key things here. First, you will be tired after giving such close scrutiny to your application package and this may cause you to miss some aspects of the details. Second, the people who will see your package are well- practiced skim readers . . . they read hundreds of report cards and pieces of correspondence regularly. With this exposure, spelling and grammar mistakes seem to leap off of the page as they skim. Be sure they don't find these problems in your application.

Be sure to print and examine your whole package before you submit it. This will allow you to check for spelling and grammar problems one more time but will also provide an opportunity to look at the components esthetically. Consider issues like spacing, appropriate font, consistency, margins, alignment, and separation of paragraphs. While key pages should be full of useful and relevant information, they should also contain enough separation and white space to facilitate skim reading. You may want to use some italic to support skim reading as well, but use this feature very sparingly. This also applies to bold fonts.

Your Professional Signature

Your signature leaves an impression. Examine your usual signature to ensure that it is appropriate, readable, but also mature and flowing. Signatures that look like childish script may cause readers to question your maturity and suitability for the job. It is worth the time to practise your signature, as it is the only really personal impression you will provide on your cover letter.

Some Final Words about Your Resume and Cover Letter

You can't get the job if you can't get an interview. This harsh reality should put perspective on how important it is to address completion of your resume and cover letter with great care. The most impressive application documents are clear, brief, and free from errors in information, spelling, and grammar. Information is organized in a way that is expected by employers. The structure and flow of each document helps potential employers see what you can offer to their organization without having to search for ways to give an applicant the benefit of any doubt. Information is easily accessible, easy to read, skims readily, and makes every word count.

This is the type of application package that will help you get that important phone call inviting you to an interview.

CHAPTER 4

DRESS FOR THE ROLE

It is a cause for celebration when you get an invitation to your first teaching interview. You have gotten this invitation because potential employers have been convinced by your application that you can do the job and will love the job.

The interview is your opportunity to remind the employer of these two things and to convince them that they will love working with you. You will have about 25 minutes to address this final essential part of the fit between their needs and your skills.

Dressing for the interview is a crucial part of making the best possible impression in that precious 25 minutes! Remember, teaching is a conservative profession. Your choice of dress for the interview needs to project your understanding of the climate of the profession while providing some indication of your personality. Make your choices very carefully.

An easy guideline for interviews is to wear a suit. However, the guideline doesn't work if the weather is hot and humid and in a school office, which is unlikely to be air-conditioned. Looking wilted at an interview is unlikely to impress anyone. So, what do you wear?

A general rule of thumb is to choose darker colours such as navy blue or black for main pieces of clothing. Generally, the more elevated the position you are applying for, the darker your wardrobe should be. However, you want to balance this a bit to reflect your age and your gender. Small, tasteful accessories with a bit of colour are suitable but you have to be strategic and cautious not to overdue it.

Here are some general guidelines that address both gender and weather variables.

Interview Attire for Women

For women, choose dark pants or a dark straight skirt, a lighter blouse, and a matching or contrasting jacket with a solid fabric or subtle pattern (e.g., tweed). Avoid large, bold patterns such as a paisley. If you choose a skirt, be sure skirt length is at the knee or longer. Avoid soft, flowing fabrics and wider skirts. If you choose to wear dress pants instead of a skirt, be sure the pants are not too tight.

Keep jewelry minimal and avoid jewelry that will make noise that could be distracting during your interview (e.g., bangles). If you wear earrings, choose small studs and avoid earrings that dangle. If you usually wear several rings, select one or two for this occasion.

Makeup should be minimal and tastefully applied. Avoid heavy eye makeup and bright lipsticks.

Your hair should be styled to suit your age but be aware of how you may show your nervousness by touching your hair. I know of women who have lost important positions because they fussed with their hair throughout an interview. Hair tossing, strand pulling, and even putting the ends of hair in your mouth are all behaviours I have seen in nervous interviewees. As you can imagine, some of these behaviours do not inspire confidence in a professional teacher! In fact, interviewers can be so distracted by these behaviours that they don't really hear how you answer their questions. They are probably busy imagining how these behaviours will impact parents when they meet you as their child's new teacher! If you choose to clip your hair back, choose a smaller sized clip that won't draw attention.

Interviewers are likely to check your footwear when you enter or exit the interview room. Wear flats or low-heeled shoes, in a dark colour. This is not the place for high heels or risking a fall as you walk. Be sure your shoes are clean and polished. Some interviewers may see your choice of footwear as a reflection of your sensible choices and your awareness of the culture of schools. While you may not see this as fair, you need to be aware that it may be the reality of the workplace.

Choosing the right top is probably the most important dress decision you will make. Remember that teaching is a conservative profession. To present yourself well in this context, choose a conservative blouse to go under a dark dress jacket. The blouse should be one that you can wear without the jacket if the weather or the interview room become uncomfortably warm. Choose a solid colour or a muted pattern in soft colours. Select a blouse that has sleeves (short, three quarters, or long, depending on the season), and a collar. Button up the front of the blouse or top, leaving no more than one button undone.

Do not use perfume or body splash scents for an interview. Increasingly, people are sensitive to these scents and, in a small room when you may be nervous, the scents can be overpowering. Similarly, remove any visible body piercing jewelry and cover any tattoos. Also, do not go into an interview smelling of cigarette smoke. The smell of clean clothes and freshly washed hair will work in your favour.

A purse can be an awkward accessory at an interview. If you decide to take a purse, follow these hints for managing it before and during the interview. Take a smaller sized purse in a colour that matches your shoe colour. Carry it over your left shoulder as you enter the interview room. This will leave your right hand free to shake hands with interviewers if necessary (we'll revisit this idea later), without having the awkward pause while you shuffle a purse out of your right hand. When you arrive in the interview room, place your purse on the floor to your left of the seat that is provided for interviewees. Never place your purse on the interview table. This surface should only be used for items related to the interview.

If you take your Professional Portfolio with you to the interview, you need to manage it the way you would for any other accessory. Carry it in your left hand to leave your right hand clear for shaking without awkward pauses. We'll consider how you should use your portfolio during the interview later in Chapters 6 and 7.

Interview Attire for Men

In many ways the interview attire choices for men are much easier than those for women. Select a dark coloured, tailored suit. Be sure it is freshly cleaned and pressed. Select a light coloured shirt and a complimentary tie.

If the weather is particularly warm, a suit jacket and tie are optional. Instead, select a short-sleeved shirt of a conservative, solid colour. White or pastel colours work best. If you wear any jewelry, make it minimal (e.g., a watch).

As was recommended for women applicants, **do not** use cologne or body splash scents for an interview. Increasingly, people are sensitive to these scents and, in a small room when you may be nervous, the scents can be overpowering. Similarly, remove any visible body piercing jewelry and cover any tattoos. Also, do not go into an interview smelling of cigarette smoke. The smell of clean clothes and freshly washed hair will work in your favour.

Keep accessories to a minimum. A watch is suitable but think carefully before wearing any other jewelry items. Be sure your shoes are dress shoes, and that they are clean and polished. If you take a professional portfolio to the interview, carry it in your left hand so that you do not need to shuffle it around to shake hands at the start of your interview.

A fresh haircut always leaves a good impression. It tells potential employers that you recognize the importance of this interview and respect the time they are giving you enough to make a special effort. Always be clean-shaven for an interview. Facial hair (e.g., mustache, beard) should be neatly trimmed.

Dressing to Impress

I have already said earlier that you won't get a second chance to make a good first impression. While it may seem superficial and somewhat shallow to focus so much on what you wear to an interview, try to put yourself in the shoes of the interviewer. Aside from what you have written about yourself in your application package, they have very little, if any, other information to judge you in comparison to other applicants. Your dress and grooming will give them the first personal clues about your suitability for the position. They are trying to imagine how parents and students will perceive you when they meet you for the first time.

You have all heard the phrase, "Dress for success". This applies to every interview you attend. Similarly, while nobody expects you to dress formally every day you are working in a school, you should be ever mindful of how you dress in a professional context. While some say you should dress for practice teaching as you see other teachers dress, we question if that is the best advice. There will be several people at the interview table. While some of them may be teachers, you know for sure that at least one of them will be the school principal. It seems wise to me to take your daily dress code cues from the one person whom you know for certain will be at the table!

Since we all build our professional reputations from every contact we have with students and other professionals, remember that every minute you are in the schools for any purpose is in reality a part of the interview process. If you try to be vigilant about always presenting your best self in these professional contexts, including by how you dress, you will make good decisions about how you dress for success. You may also find that with some age groups of students, they will admire and even imitate your choices in school dress.

Finally, be sure that you are aware of dress codes that may be in place in some jurisdictions. While a dress code is not intended as a policy against certain types of materials, or as a judgment on someone's taste, it is wise to be aware of perceptions . . . they are someone's reality!

Dressing wisely for the interview opportunity is a way to make the strong impression you want to make so that you have an opportunity during the interview to convince employers that you are the right fit for their needs.

CHAPTER 5

KNOWING WHO WILL INTERVIEW YOU

Interview teams for teaching positions are made up differently for different purposes and to reflect the demands and timelines that are relevant at different times of the year. It is important to know who will be interviewing you because interviewers will each have their own set of priorities which they bring to their role as interviewer. These priorities will be evident in the interview process either in the questions that are asked or in the way that the interviewer interprets and values various aspects of your answer. If an interviewer has a set of "listen for" criteria pre-established for each question they ask in an interview, they are likely to be attentive to those key words as you speak. They may even have a checklist of ideas to listen for in your answers and may be checking these off of a list as you answer.

A priorities "listen for" list may be designed like the example below:

Question	Listen for	Interviewer Notes
Tell us about yourself as a teacher.	• academic qualifications	
	• beliefs about learning	
	• optimizing students' learning	
	• differentiated instruction	
	• differentiated assessment	
	• active learning	
	• student engagement	
	• positive, supportive learning environment	

- openness to personal and professional growth
- openess to obtaining additional qualifications

A priorities "listen for" list may be designed by the interview team or by the principal in charge of the team ahead of the interview time and given to the interview team before you enter the room. If the interview is for a system position such as a supply teacher list, then the list may be made up ahead of time by a system committee and it would then be provided for the interview team.

It would help your interview preparation if you anticipate interview questions using the process that a systems committee would go through to develop a priorities "listen for" list. In Chapters 7, 8 and 9, much more detail will be provided about the types and structures of interview questions you should expect.

Even though a well prepared interview team is likely to have a priorities list to guide their assessment of your responses to the interview questions, each member of the team is still an individual who brings their prior experience to their role as an interviewer. Each interviewer will still filter your responses through their own knowledge of teaching and their own perception of the needs of their school and the system as a whole. This is why it will be helpful for you to know who is interviewing you.

In some systems, you may be able to call the Human Resources Department before your interview and get the exact names and positions of the interviewers. In other systems, this information may not be shared with interviewees. However, even if authorities at the school board level are reluctant to share specific names of interviewers, they may still be able to help you prepare by telling you the positions of the people who will attend your interview. This information will help you focus answers to the questions to address likely background and priorities of the interviewers.

In general, interview teams are likely to be structured differently for system positions than for school-based positions.

System positions (e.g., the supply teacher list) => 3 or more principals/vice-principals; may include a human resources staff member who is there to monitor process only;

School-based positions => the school principal and two or more teachers; the teachers usually include the special education resource teacher and one teacher from the division (elementary) or the department (secondary).

Many school boards have a policy that requires that at least three people serve on each interview team. This practice helps the board protect itself against claims of unfair hiring or breach of human rights statutes.

If school-based hiring needs to happen during times when teachers might not normally be in the school (e.g., during winter or summer holiday breaks) principals often support each other by forming hiring teams from among their colleagues. In this instance, even a school-based hiring team could be made up of three or more principals.

Knowing More About an Interviewer's Perspective

Each of us brings our past life and career experiences to bear on our decisions. These experiences are what have created our personal set of priorities, interests, values, and assumptions. This is also true of interview team members. Regardless of the pre-interview preparation they may have undertaken as an interview team, each member of the team will also have a personal perspective on each candidate for the role they are seeking to fill. Before you interview for a position, it is wise to consider the various perspectives each interviewer may have. In this way, you can plan to broaden the scope of your responses to each question so that you address each interview team member's priorities in each of your responses.

While this may seem like a tall order and somewhat like trying to read minds, it will also be probable that key phrases that you use in your responses will resonate with several members of your interview committee, regardless of their perspective and past experiences. Some phrases are just expected of a well-informed applicant.

However, these are some general guidelines you should keep in mind about your interview team's perspectives and requirements of applicants.

School principals hiring for the system level supply teachers' list will want to know that you are:

- reliable
- prompt
- respectful of students
- strong with regard to your classroom management approaches
- committed to the system (e.g., not likely to leave as soon as you are initiated into the system's way of operating)
- able and willing to communicate with parents as you meet them in your supply teacher role
- willing to take on supplemental tasks of the day (e.g., marking, extra supervision, coaching, etc.)
- able to take direction from other teachers
- available when needed

School principals hiring for a school-based positions will want to know that you are:

- appropriately qualified to meet the needs of the position
- well informed about school and system priorities
- respectful of students and parents
- knowledgeable about how to improve students' learning
- able to differentiate curriculum and assessment to support students' success
- willing and able to work as part of their school team
- committed to constant improvement in your professional practice
- able to take direction and grow professionally
- able to resolve conflicts productively
- committed to ensuring student engagement

The main filter for the principals when they are considering you for hiring is, "Can you do the job?" Secondarily, they may also be considering if you are likely to commit to the system and school once you have the job. They do not want to invest time and money to continue your professional training and then find that you plan to move to another system. So, they may also be considering the question, "Will you love the job?" They know that if they can hire a person who will love their job, their whole staff will be a happier team.

When teachers are part of the hiring team they are also considering if you can do the job. But, they are strongly invested in their school and their students so they are also placing their priority on ensuring that they will be able to work cooperatively with the people they hire. They are giving some priority to the question, "Will we love working with you?" Teacher participants on a hiring team are placing priority on your:

- ability to do the job well
- respect for their experience and expertise
- ability to take direction and grow professionally
- ability to work with a team
- ability to avoid or resolve conflicts productively
- ability to recognize the contributions of other professionals to the school's achievements
- commitment to common goals
- ability to think like a teacher
- commitment to the profession and the union that governs your employment conditions

When a special education resource teacher is part of the school-based hiring team, this person brings the specialization of their role in the school to bear on the interview. In the school, this person specializes in ensuring that the needs of special learners are met. The special education resource teacher interviewer, in addition to being a teacher looking for someone they can work with well, will also be considering your:

- ability to demonstrate understanding of strategies to differentiate instruction and assessment

- ability to promote active, engaging learning
- understanding of different forms of special needs among learners
- ability to focus instructional efforts on meeting learners' needs
- ability to manage the documentation needed to track learners' progress individually

All of these perspectives will be brought to bear on the answers you give in interviews. It is therefore critical that you understand how to prepare thoroughly for the high stakes time you will have in the interview.

Understanding "Fit"

"Fit" refers to the idea that the person applying for the job is monitored for their ability to fill the needs of the employer. Fit theory has many aspects of fit that operate together to see the needs of the employer filled by the skills of the employee. Following is some further background about the theory of fit.

The quality of classroom teachers is regarded as a key factor in the success of students (OECD, 2004, 2005; Rivkin, Hanushek, & Kain, 2005). While factors such as the school climate may relate to the student's success with academic progress, the impact of the teacher is a higher influential factor in determining who succeeds and who may not (Dinham, Ingvarson, & Kleinhenz, 2008). These acknowledgements highlight the crucial nature of effective hiring practices to ensure the most effective teachers are hired (Walsh & Tracy, 2004). Increasingly, those who hire teachers look to ensure effective hiring strategies to increase the chances of improving student success (OECD, 2004; 2005). Efforts to improve hiring practices are based on the recognition that individual teachers matter when student success is the goal.

Through hiring practices within various school boards, those charged with hiring can reasonably be assumed to be trying to ensure that they hire the most effective teachers and that interviews and adjunctive filtering strategies for hiring have some criteria that support this selection process. These criteria may be stated in policy documents in the jurisdiction and may identify selection criteria and retention supports (Young, Levin, & Wallin, 2007). In school systems, ensuring that decision makers can hire strong teachers and then support their continuous growth once they are in the profession, are seen as crucial ways to leverage student success (Darling-Hammond, 2001; 2003;Harris, 2004).

However, it may be that those who are responsible for hiring effective teachers for school jurisdictions or for individual schools may face a problematic situation. They may lack local or jurisdictional policies to guide their selection process and may therefore be guided by personal perceptions, idiosyncratic assessments, and relatively unacknowledged value judgments (Cranston, 2012). Additionally, hiring individuals or hiring teams may have competing conceptions of teacher effectiveness (Little, Goe, & Bell, 2009). Since, defining an effective teacher is a subjective and interpretive act (Cochran-Smith and Power, 2010; Rabinowicz & Travers, 1953) and there may be little consensus on the usefulness of a narrow definition of teacher effectiveness (Campbell, Kyriakides, Muijs, & Robinson, 2003), those charged with hiring effective teachers may disagree about what effectiveness is in their context.

Also, there is no known method of consistently predicting the effectiveness of a teacher in the classroom once they are hired (Cashin, 1994). However, there is general agreement among many researchers that a teacher's actual classroom performance may have some predictive value relative to their future successes in the classroom (Bill and Melinda Gates Foundation, 2010; Gladwell, 2008; Goldhaber & Hansen, 2010; Jacob & Lefgren, 2006). Since many jurisdictions rely solely on an interview to identify the most promising teachers, many jurisdictions train their hiring personnel to use performance-based interviewing techniques to structure questions that bridge the gap between past practice and future practices. By improving the screening and selection of teachers, jurisdictions attempt to improve the cadre of employees who show most promise that they will leverage student achievement by being effective in the classroom (Darling-Hammond & Berry,

1999; OECD, 2004;2005: Wise, Darling-Hammond & Berry, 1997). This is essentially an effort to match the organizational needs with the available talents of applicants and the demands of an effective teacher's role (Herriot, 1989; Montgomery, 1996; Plumbley, 1985; Zhu & Dowling, 2002). Finding this match often boils down to the search for strategies that help organizations identify the most promising teacher qualities (Cochran-Smith & Power, 2010) which is problematic if jurisdictions fail to use a systematic, research-based approach to the hiring practices they rely heavily upon as they make such high stakes decisions (Boyd, Goldhaber, Lankford, & Wyckoff, 2007; Walsh & Tracy, 2004).

Current hiring practices may further be highly problematic in two key ways. First, those seeking to be hired may be unaware of how to prepare for hiring and how to anticipate the needs of various jurisdictions, leaving them unaware of how to improve their prospects of obtaining their first teaching position (Ontario College of Teachers, 2011). Second, evidence that school jurisdictions make effective decisions about whom they hire in the selection of teachers is largely unavailable (Boyd et al, 2007).

The tension between the use of objective criteria for hiring (Harris, Rutledge, Ingle, & Thompson, 2007) and the subjective practice of hiring based on interviews and references may confuse the issue of trying to ensure that the most effective teachers ultimately get to teach. When subjective approaches are used exclusively, the high stakes task of hiring the most effective teachers may rely on a faulty assumption; that those responsible for hiring can successfully identify the candidates' characteristics by the means available in their jurisdiction (Kristof-Brown, Zimmerman, & Johnson, 2005). Additionally, some research shows that school-based hiring may provide those charged with the task of hiring teachers with the better teachers (Darling-Hammond, 1997; DeArmond, Gross, & Goldhaber, 2010). School-based hiring allows principals to select teachers whose characteristics they perceive to fit the school and its needs and thereby support the desired school culture (Deal & Peterson, 1999; Firestone & Louis, 1999). But, in many jurisdictions, administrators hire for system positions and may have little say in who is assigned to their school.

Fullan (2011) suggests that hiring jurisdictions need to use approaches that are both systemic and consistent for the task of hiring teachers. Some jurisdictions are addressing this approach by developing multi-staged selection processes for teachers that attempt to find the best fit among teacher candidates (Pappano, 2011). This trend is being referred to as *predictive hiring*. Predictive hiring addresses the conversation about educational improvement by attempting to predict the best teachers by hiring smarter, thereby flagging problematic fits during a multi-staged selection process. Predictive hiring attempts to buttress the traditional resume, application letter, and interview triad for selection with the addition of further filters that may provide better or broader data on which to make a teacher hiring decision. Predictive hiring approaches can include: an initial phone interview; the observation of a model lesson taught by the teacher applicant; a face-to-face interview; a problem-solving email exercise (e.g., responding to an angry parent); and, a professional task simulation (e.g., a student achievement data analysis). Predictive hiring practices may seek to provide a best teacher fit that includes a fit between the applicant and the work environment, the job requirements, the organization/school and its culture, and the group with whom they will work (Anderson, Lievens, van Dam, & Ryan, 2004; Antonioni & Park, 2001; Ehrhart & Makransky, 2007; Kristof-Brown et al, 2005; Sekiguchi, 2004), with some indication that assessments of fit between the applicant and the organizational culture seem to predominate in hiring decisions (Karren & Graves, 1994).

While the need for highly effective teachers is a given, identifying what makes the teacher effective is not. Similarly, how highly effective teachers are chosen in the selection process can be problematic. Theories about optimizing human capital (Schultz, 1961) to get the best fit of candidate to needs may be more subjective than is productive, and predictive approaches to hiring, while showing some promise of positive yields, are yet to be proven and are labour intensive to implement. However, if jurisdictions could engage in the intense process of identifying the key characteristics they want to see in their teachers to ensure their effectiveness in supporting students' learning, we hypothesize that hiring practices and their high stakes outcomes will be strengthened.

These key characteristics are the characteristics of "fit" that employers seek to uncover when they interview teacher candidates. In well-situated and strategic hiring organizations, interviews will try to assess the fit between:

- the applicant and the work environment;
- the applicant's skills and the job requirements;
- the applicant's beliefs and values and the organization/ school and its culture;
- the applicant's social skills and the group with whom he/ she will work; and
- the applicant's skills and values and the needs of the supervisor.

Fit theory also can be understood using the terms of the three key questions that were identified earlier:

- ***Can you do the job?*** - the applicant and the work environment; the applicant's skills and the job requirements
- ***Will you love the job?*** - the applicant's beliefs and values and the organization/school and its culture
- ***Will we love working with you?*** - the applicant's social skills and the group with whom he/she will work; and the applicant's skills and values and the needs of the supervisor.

Practising and Preparing for the Interview

There are many online sources of information about teaching interviews that may be helpful to you as you prepare. You will need to be a critical consumer of these sites but you may find that some will give you further perspective and opportunities to practise analyzing examples of interview questions and interview clips.

The following sites are provided as helpful examples:

Note:
Many of these sites require updated versions of Adobe Flash Player.

EducationCanada.com

http://resource.educationcanada/i_tips1.html

This site contains some strong links that take you through the interview process from beginning to end.

About.com.JobSearching

http://jobsearch.about.com/od/interviewquestionsanswers/a/teacherint.htm

This site contains a number of links on the sidebar to *you tube* examples of candidates answering interview questions. This would be a useful site to view and critique for ways to align or diversify your responses from the way they are done in the video.

Getting Hired: Teacher Interview(Elementary)

http://www.youtube.com/watch?v=El7QdW1Myk8&feature=related

Although this is an American scenario and the interviewer does some things that skilled interviewers will not do (e.g., talking too much, being excessive with praise) the interviewee does give some structure to her answers that may help with your preparation. What she does really well is transition from the interviewer's comments to her responses.

Also, this site has several sidebar links to other aspects of interviewing that are valuable to consider as you prepare.

The single key message of this chapter is this. The interview, as it is presently used in most teacher hiring situations, is a very brief but very high stakes process. You need to be well prepared for every interview you are given. Each interview should add to your skill as an interviewee so you should always be prepared to be reflective and critical about your participation in an interview, whether you get the job or not. Even when you are hired, it is likely that you will go through several interviews for promotion or job reassignment while you are in the profession so it is always wise to learn as much as you can about how the process works.

When employers face situations where more teachers are available than may be needed in the job market, they can afford to be particularly strident and diligent in their efforts to get the best teacher fit for the job. As hiring a teacher is a big investment for a school board, often initiating a relationship that lasts more than 30 years, and as unions become ever stronger in defending teachers, it may be that we will see changes in hiring practices. Employers may begin to place less emphasis on the teaching interview and may use other elements of *predictive hiring* to compliment this aspect of the process. However, it seems likely that some type of face-to-face interviewing will continue to be part of the process so it is wise to learn as much as you can about its variations in different contexts.

CHAPTER 6

READ THE ROOM: YOU ONLY HAVE ONE CHANCE TO MAKE A GOOD FIRST IMPRESSION!

Congratulations! You are already a success because you've been invited to an interview in a very competitive work environment. If you have prepared well for your interview, you should be prepared to make a good first impression as you start your interview. As the title of this chapter says, you only have one chance to make a good first impression. Another way to say this same thing is that you'll never get a second chance to make a good first impression!

There are many things you can do to make sure that your first impression is a positive and sustained one. This chapter will give you some guidelines about how to make the impression you want right from the beginning of your interview.

When you are contacted about an interview, do these things to make sure you have the details you may need. First, record the name and position of the person who calls you. Take their phone number. Although it is unlikely that you would ever have to cancel your interview, life has a way of getting in the way when it's most inconvenient. If you become ill or have a family circumstance that makes it impossible for you to attend the interview, you should contact the interviewer or their designated contact person as soon as possible. Second, ask the contact person who will be interviewing you and what their positions are. Make a record of these names and positions as you listen so that you have access to this information as you prepare for the interview. Third, confirm the location of the interview and write it down. While you are still on the phone, repeat the location of the interview to the contact person. These are vital details that are all too easy to forget in the excitement of getting that call.

Before the day of the interview, drive or walk to the location. The day of the interview is not the day to try to figure out where to go. If you know where to go and how to get there prior to the interview day, this will help you to relax on the day of the interview.

It is likely that there will be a reception area in the board office or school where you will be interviewed. When you arrive at the interview, announce yourself if there is a receptionist. This person will direct you to a spot where you will wait until you are called into the interview.

Timing Your Arrival

Part of making that critically positive first impression is very easy to accomplish. Arrive early. Almost every aspect of a teacher's day is scheduled to coordinate with other people and with spaces in the school. When you arrive early for your interview, aside from transmitting the message that you understand this circumstance, this will communicate your enthusiasm and help you to compose yourself before you are called in to start your interview. The chance to take a few deep breathes before your interview starts will help you appear composed and unflustered during the critical first few moments of your time in the interview room.

I recommend that you arrive about 30 minutes earlier than your scheduled interview time. There are several advantages to this. If you are early you can take a few minutes for a visit to a washroom to take a final look at your attire and check your appearance. Don't take anything into the interview that you don't need for the interview. So, hang up your coat and leave boots behind. Bring indoor shoes and get changed into them. Turn your cell phone off (better yet, leave it in your car!).

Arriving early also allows you the advantage of being able to see other interviewees who may be coming out of the interview room. It may help to calm you if you see other people coming out of the interview being relaxed and smiling. I have also had previous interviewees come out of an interview and immediately start to share questions they were surprised by in their interview. While this may work to your advantage, it is not wise to be seen to be discussing this by the interviewers. Instead, just listen if the previous interviewee needs to talk.

Some interviewees may also find it helpful to take a copy of your resume to review before the interview, as you wait. For some, this practice may boost confidence and refresh memories of instances you may want to mention in the interview.

Meeting the Interviewers

Interview teams will typically designate one member of the team to be the greeter who will come and find you in the reception room and escort you to the interview room. As soon as you see this person, your interview has started.

When the greeting member of the interview team approaches you in the reception room, stand up. Offer your right hand to shake. Hold your portfolio in your left hand. As the interviewer shakes your hand, listen carefully to how they introduce themselves. If they use their first name, echo that as you greet them (e.g., "Hello Rick. How are you?"). If they introduce themselves using a title, that is how you should echo in your greeting (e.g., "Hello Mr. Martin. How are you?"). Smile and make eye contact as you shake hands.

Practise your Handshake!

The wet fish handshake does not support a good first impression. We have all had people who have shaken our hands with limp fingers, damp with nervous perspiration. We all have the same negative reaction to this. Be sure your hands are dry, your grip is firm, your hand release is quick (a few seconds . . . but take your cue from the other person), and you make eye contact as you shake hands. Smile!

Be Prepared for Small Talk

An interview is all about business, and business is all about getting the job done. However, in an interview context, there will a brief time at the outset where the formal interview has not yet started but people are still getting settled in preparation. This is a time when someone on the interview team may have a casual comment to make. The purposes of these comments are to bridge awkward silences and help you feel welcomed and relaxed. They are ice breakers.

Be careful how you engage these comments. Avoid overly casual comments, talking too much about a passing comment, poorly placed laughs, or inappropriate humour. Be agreeable and polite but be prepared to move on. The chair of the committee will start the formal part of the interview as soon as they can.

Greeting the Interviewers

When you enter the interview room, the interview team is likely to be there already and they are likely seated around an interview table. Most interview teams will favour a round table or a short oblong one where they can place you at the end of the table. This allows all interviewers to have an equally easy view of you during your interview. As you enter the room scan it quickly, making eye contact with each interviewer. Do not sit until you are asked to do so and directed to a specific seat.

As you enter the room, the interviewers will do one of two things. They will either stand or they won't. Both of these behaviours are giving you a message. If they do stand, they are inviting you to introduce yourself and shake hands with each person. If they do not stand, they are saying that they want to skip that formality and start directly into the interview questions.

If the interviewers introduce themselves, pay attention to how they name themselves (e.g., by first name or title). As you respond to their greetings, use their name as they present it in your greeting response (e.g., "Hello Michelle" or "Hello Dr. Denning"). Stand until you are directed where to sit. This will usually be done by the person who has met you in the reception room. Often, the interviewee's chair will be the one closest to the door.

As you sit, set your portfolio to your side with the labeled spine facing the interviewers. Even if you do not get a chance to use your portfolio in your interview, placing it on the table tells interviewers that you have come prepared. Ladies, if you brought a purse, place it on the floor to your left. Do not put it on the interview table. Settle into the chair with your back straight and your feet planted straight under your knees. Lean forward slightly. This posture says that you're eager and you are open to ideas.

Using your Hands During an Interview

The way you use your hands during an interview is a critical aspect of creating the positive impression you want to make. Use of your hands can support your enthusiasm and make some ideas of your presentation memorable. However, overuse of your hands can leave the impression that you are nervous and can distract interviewers. When you first sit down, fold your hands together on the table in front of you. This will help you be aware of your hands and how you are using them and it will also force you to lean into the table to give the enthusiastic body language you want to convey.

If you use your hands to explain or emphasize an idea, do this sparingly. Think of your hand space as being the spot directly in front of you but contained within the small square between your waist and chin, and between your shoulders. This will help you avoid overly exaggerated gestures. Always return your hands to the neutral, resting position folded on the table in front of you after your key point has been made. Be sure that your resting place for your hands is rested! Avoid a white knuckled grip that will transmit your nervousness.

Be aware of any tendency you may have to use your hands when you are nervous. Avoid tapping on the table.

Leaning in and Leaning Out

Your body language during your interview is a critical method for communicating with potential employers. You need to use it strategically to get the greatest, most positive impact from it. As you start each answer, lean into the table slightly. This will cause the interviewers to focus on you and to note your enthusiasm and engagement. As you conclude each answer, support your concluding statements by leaning away from the table slightly. This is a subtle indicator that your answer is coming to a close and causes listeners to focus on your concluding statements.

Monitor your own nervous tendencies as you practise this leaning. Be sure to avoid slouching, tapping your legs, frequent changes in hand positions, or touching your face or hair. Avoid being overly casual by putting your hands behind your head. Watch out to avoid banging your hands on the edge of the table as you use them to emphasize an idea.

Pacing

In Chapters 8, 9, and 10 we will address specific structures and content for interview questions. However, all answers will be strengthened by modulating the pace of your presentation. Don't race through answers. Be sure to structure the answers as you planned initially and close each answer confidently. Modulate your voice to emphasize ideas and to close the final sentence in your response.

By using natural conversational pacing, modulating your voice, emphasizing key ideas through voice and occasionally through gestures, and leaning away from the table when you are ending your answer, you will maintain strong communication with the interviewers and continue to impress them with your ability to build relationships in short time spans.

Eye Contact

Eye contact is an important and effective way to make sure that you are building a relationship with your interviewers. This is not easy to do in the very short 25 minutes allowed for most interviews. Once you have made the initial eye contact when you entered the room, you will need to focus on maintaining eye contact and building on the initial connection by using eye contact throughout the interview.

Interview questions are dispersed to the interviewee in one of two ways. Either one person will ask all of the questions or the questions will be distributed among the interviewers and they will rotate as the interview progresses. Regardless of how the questioning is dispersed, you will need to make sure to make ongoing eye contact with each interviewer throughout the interview.

There is sometimes a downside to making good eye contact. If you are connecting well with your interview team, one or more members of the team may feel that they need to respond to the invitation of positive eye contact. An interviewer may nod at you as you speak. This can be very encouraging but you need to be very cautious not to misread the message they are giving you. Your interviewers want you to be successful and a nod should be seen as encouragement. However, you can be taken off track by the nods. Be careful not to read the nods as "Give us more of that". It should be interpreted as "Good. Stay on track." Be sure you stick to your plan for the answer to this topic and don't get taken off topic by someone's interest in one point.

In a practice session, you may want to monitor, or even videotape your own mannerisms to make sure that you make suitable eye contact during an interview.

Be aware of eye mannerisms that may not work in your favour:

- Avoid rolling your eyes when recounting or explaining an idea.
- Avoid fluttering your eyelids; this may convey nervousness.
- Eye contact is essential to establish trust and make connections with your interview team; disperse eye contact among all members of the interview team without over-focusing on one person.
- When you need a moment to think, breathe in and look down. If you stare straight up during times when you need to pause, interviewers may see this as an indication of insincerity.
- Make your eye contact casual rather than fixed, as with a stare. Spread the eye contact around among the interviewers as the interview progresses.

By making effective eye contact you build a relationship with your interviewers and they build a commitment to your success.

Closing Your Interview

Many teaching interviews are designed to include 5 to 7 questions and take up about 25 minutes of a 30-minute interview time slot. We will talk in much more detail about interview structures and questions in Chapters 8, 9, and 10. However, before we talk about specific questions that may be asked, you should be aware of how to end your interview in a way that maintains the strong first impression that you established at the beginning of your interview.

After all questions have been asked and answered, the chairperson of the interview committee, who will almost always be a principal, will indicate that your interview is over. He/she may make some closing comments about when their decision will be made and what will happen next.

This is an important decision for you, so you will be anxious to know their decision. However, you should avoid any tendency to ask for timelines or impressions. Instead, close your interview with a short, appreciative comment. For example, you might say, "Thank you. I have appreciated your time today" or "Thank you for the opportunity to speak to you in this interview". Don't forget to smile on your way out of the room. Once again, carry your portfolio in your left hand and be prepared to shake hands with the interviewers if they stand and offer that opportunity.

By managing these aspects of your interview carefully, you can be sure to make the powerful first impression you want.

CHAPTER 7

KNOW HOW INTERVIEWS ARE STRUCTURED: EXPECTING THE STYLE OF QUESTIONS YOU MAY GET

You may have heard that sports trainers often use visualization to help athletes imagine the competition situations they will face. This is done to help athletes become more comfortable with the range of possibilities they may face in competition. In many ways, preparing for an interview is much the same as learning to visualize in preparation for competition. If you know more about how a typical interview operates, and what you can expect, you can relax about the process and focus on the content of your responses to interview questions.

We have already considered how you should apply for teaching positions, prepare for the documents that are needed in an application, dress for an interview, and accept an invitation to be interviewed. This chapter will focus on how questions in interviews may be shaped. Then, Chapter 8 will talk more about the types of questions you may face in an interview.

Assessing your Interviewers

"Assessing your Interviewers" may sound a little backwards to you. Interviews, after all, are about assessing you. This chapter will explain why it is critical for you to think about assessing who is interviewing you as well.

The problem you face as a person being interviewed is that all interviewers do not have the same experience interviewing others and they may have little or no formal training in how to conduct an interview. That creates problems for you in the interview because the group of interviewers may be coming into the interview with totally different sets of beliefs about their roles. They may also have totally different sets of goals for hiring.

While the interview team is presented to you as a team, in reality they may have had very little time as a group to establish common goals, common visions, and commonly agreed to questions. If the position you are applying for is a system position, the interview team may have been given the questions from another source such as the superintendent or the Human Resources staff. If the questions are for a school-based position, it is possible that the principal may have been the only member of the interview team to develop or vet the questions prior to the interview.

In the best possible scenario, the members of the interview team will be trained interviewers, with a common vision, who have time to cooperatively develop the interview questions and cooperatively develop a set of indicators or "listen-fors" that they want to hear in ideal responses. As this process takes quite a lot of time and resources, it is less common than may be desirable. More research into hiring practices and interview preparations may help school boards and administrators realize the value of strong preparation for these teacher-hiring interviews. After all, if they make a mistake in their hiring, the impact of the mistake could last for well over thirty years.

In a more common scenario, the members of the interview team will not have any interview training. There may be a clear system mission that all interviewers are aware of but they may have lacked opportunities to come to agreement about the critical questions that should be asked during an interview. They may also lack clarity about what aspects of your answer may provide an indication of your knowledge and skills.

In the worst-case scenario, you may have an unpredictable mix of the two situations described above. Your interview team may have members with training and without training, with and without experience developing interview questions, with and without a common view of what they are looking for in a good teacher, and with no follow-up commitment to the teacher who is hired if that person is hired for a system position.

This worst-case scenario is a problem for you as the interviewee because it can result in some hastily prepared interview questions that evolve from some very different beliefs about interviewing, and provide little guidance for you about how they expect you to answer the question.

Acing the Worst-Case Scenario

Regardless of the background in interviewing of your interview team, you need to understand and manage any of the three interview scenarios that you may face. Interviewers will come from one of two orientations. They will either believe:

- that the person being interviewed can imagine a described situation and explain *what they would do* as a teacher to address the situation

  OR

- that the person being interviewed has some experience to prepare for this job and can describe *what they have done* to respond to the situation.

When questions are designed to have applicants describe what they would do, we call this "crystal ball questions". You may or may not have experienced this situation. When questions are designed to focus on describing what you have done, this approach is commonly called *performance based or competency-based interviewing.* Performance based interviewing has evolved from the belief that the best predictor of future performance is past performance. This is different from the predictive hiring we discussed earlier in this book because performance based interviewing still relies heavily on analyzing your question responses and does not typically involve any tasks outside of the interview.

The problem for you as the person being interviewed is that you may have people from both sets of orientations on the same committee. This could mean that the questions could be designed from a mixture of these two approaches. Later, you will learn how to handle this in an interview.

Written Components in Interviews

Some school boards may include a written component in their hiring interviews. The purposes of the written component(s) may vary with the job.

If the job is a classroom teaching position, interviewers are trying to obtain a sample of your writing as an indicator of your problem solving abilities, as a way to measure your sensitivity to the issues, and as a way to assess the quality of your writing.

If the job is a second language teaching position (e.g., French, aboriginal languages, etc.) written tasks are designed to allow employers to assess your language fluency.

Optimizing the Questions by Being Strategic in Your Responses

Learning to respond to the questions in an interview is a complicated and often underestimated skill. We will address specific topics for questions in later chapters. However, regardless of the topic of the questions in your interview, your responses need to be designed to convey the strongest possible example of your knowledge and skills in the most concise way. This is not made easier for you if the questions are coming from two different orientations.

Here's what you need to do to bridge this problem. Take the question and change it into a performance-based question. Here is an example of how you can do that.

Example

Interviewer: *Tell us about what you would do if an angry parent came to see you, concerned about the homework you are giving. What will you do?*

In your mind, change this question to the following:

Interviewer*:   Tell us about a time when you had to deal with an angry parent (e.g., concern about homework). What happened? What did you do? What did you learn from the outcome? How will this experience affect your next experience of this type?*

The last two parts of the reframed question are critical to your ability to formulate a strong answer. Employers are always interested in knowing that you will learn from your experiences and how that learning will enrich your professional practice.

Even if questions are framed as performance based questions, you should always answer them as though the last two parts of the example question had been asked. Always consider ending your retelling of the situation by addressing, *What did you learn from the outcome? How will this experience affect your next experience of this type?* By ending your answers like this, you assure employers that you are committed to professional growth, open to improvement, and motivated to develop your skills and knowledge after you are hired.

Example

Interviewer: *Tell us about a time when you realized that a student was not progressing as expected in your classroom.*

In your mind, adjust this question to the following:

> *Tell us about a time when you realized that a student was not progressing as expected in your classroom. (e. g., What happened? What did you do? What did you learn from the outcome? How will this experience affect your next experience of this type?)*

In this example, the stem of the question that was provided by the interviewer addresses what happened and what you did about it. However, you need to enrich your answer by addressing what you learned from the outcome and what you will do in the future in a similar situation. More detail about this approach will be provided in Chapter 10.

Confidentiality and Sensitivity Issues in an Interview

Interview questions that ask you to recount experiences can be full of confidentiality pitfalls. You need to respond to the question in detail but always remember that you may ***never*** use a student's, parent's or teacher's name or other identifying details in your response.

Information about individuals is protected by the Freedom of Information and Protection of Privacy Act in Canada (often referred to as the FOI Act). While your interviewers are unlikely to know the individuals you might be tempted to speak about, they will be looking for your knowledge of the law as you answer questions. If you use names or features of the context that would allow them to identify an individual, they will have concerns about your professionalism.

Instead, in recounting incidents and situations in your answers, use terms such as "the person", "the individual", "the student", "the parent", "the teacher", "the context" to maintain a distance that respects confidentiality.

Similarly, interviewers will be looking for indications of your ability to be sensitive and empathetic to people. Be cautious to recount events in a respectful tone. Even if the question focuses on conflict, which is inherently negative, be sure to take the time in your response to express your understanding of the individual's concern and perspective and explain how you plan to accommodate that perspective in your reaction to the situation.

Structuring Your Interview Responses

As much as any other attributes you may possess, interviewers are looking for your ability to answer their questions with confidence and professionalism. When new teachers have this ability, it is seen by employers and administrators as an indicator of your ability to handle tough situations independently and successfully. When you can do this in the stressful context of an interview, they will be reassured that you will be able to handle the daily situations in a school that will benefit from your confidence and professionalism.

To project confidence and professionalism in your interview responses, each of your answers will need structure. The process of structuring your responses is much like developing an effective essay. Each answer should have three parts:

- Tell them what you're going to do.
- Do it.
- Tell them what you did.

In an essay, these parts would include an opening or thesis paragraph (Tell them what you're going to do.), a set of body paragraphs (Do it.), and a closing paragraph (Tell them what you did.). In your interview responses, these answers should be structured to do the same things.

Example

Tell them what you are going to do.

Use the opening sentences of your response to rephrase, restate, or reframe (as per performance-based interviewing) the question that was asked. Explain the framework you will use to answer the question. Lean into the table slightly as you do this.

Do it.

In 2 or 3 minutes, explain the answer to the question by explaining the situation and what you did about it. Explain what you learned from the experience and what this means about how you will handle similar situations in the future.

Tell them what you did.

Add a closing to your sentences to summarize the answer; review what you have said in a brief statement.

An example response is given below to show you how this structure will appear in an interview answer. Each of the three parts of the answer are shown in different paragraphs so that you can analyze the response as you read.

Interviewer: *Tell us about yourself as a teacher.* (This is a common opening question in an interview.)

Interviewee: *In responding to this question, I would like to tell you about my academic qualifications, my beliefs about teaching and learning, and my plans for continuous professional growth in the teaching profession.*
My academic qualifications include an honours B.A. degree with a major in English and a minor in geography. I have just completed a consecutive B. Ed. degree at XXX university with 13 weeks of practicum experience in four schools. During these practicum experiences, I had many opportunities to develop lessons that provided differentiated instruction for my students and allowed

many options for differentiated assessments for all students, including several children with identified learning challenges. I have developed expertise with technology assisted learning during my professional preparation program.

I will support learning in my classroom by engaging my students with active approaches to learning. My students will investigate issues and solve problems as they learn, through strategies that support multiple intelligences. They will have exposure to online sources of information that will be supported with strong graphic organizers to help them access the information. My students will learn in cooperative configurations that help them build their social skills and learn to appreciate and respect the perspectives of their peers and their community. My students will have opportunities to be involved in their community as leaders within the school and contributors to community events. Through safe online learning situations, I will address my students' interests by structuring their engagement in current issues that help them integrate and apply their new learning. I will help and support them as they learn new skills, and apply these skills to relevant contexts. Parents and community members will be welcomed to support and enrich our classroom learning. When visitors come to our classroom, they will enter a rich community of learners where students respect each other and engage diligently in genuine tasks that will both challenge and stimulate them. In my classroom, every student will be supported to reach and extend their potential and feel pride in their accomplishments.

I am also committed to my ongoing growth in this profession. I plan to extend and enrich my qualifications in two ways. I will enroll in a university course to acquire a certificate in XXXX. As well, I will engage in the culture of my new school(s) by becoming an active and committed member of the community of learners with the other professionals in the school and by actively seeking formal and informal mentorship from my more experienced peers in the profession. By committing to ongoing professional growth once I am hired I can ensure that I upgrade my qualifications and extend my understanding of learners and their needs.

I have tried to outline my extensive qualifications for this position, summarize my beliefs about teaching and learning by describing what you would see as my students engage in learning, and outlining my plans for continuous professional growth as a teacher and lifelong learner.

When you have finished your answer, lean back slightly in your seat to signal completion of the answer.

Using Key Words and a Positive Tone in Your Responses

It would be valuable to take the time to analyze this sample response. Some key words have been used strategically in this sample response because these words represent concepts that employers want to hear in interviews (Maynes and Hatt, 2013). Words such as "differentiated learning", "differentiated assessment", "engagement", "active learning", "problem solving", and "professional growth" will act as flags to listeners and will demonstrate your professional knowledge to them.

As you state each response, always choose to form the ideas in a positive way. Say "I will . . ." rather than "I will not". Choose active verbs and avoid words that such as "I believe". Instead, choose a more direct approach such as "I will . . ." or "I have consistently . . .".

Finally, be sure that every answer includes references to supporting, encouraging, ensuring, and responding to students' learning. This will help interviewers understand that you have made a vital professional shift in your thinking. This shift involves moving away from focusing on your teaching and moving toward focusing on your students' learning.

Focusing on Students' Learning

Our research into the traits that school administrators look for when they hire new teachers (Maynes and Hatt, 2013) shows strong agreement among those responsible for hiring about a number of characteristics that typify teachers most likely to focus on improving students' learning in their classrooms. These characteristics are identified in a diagram form below.

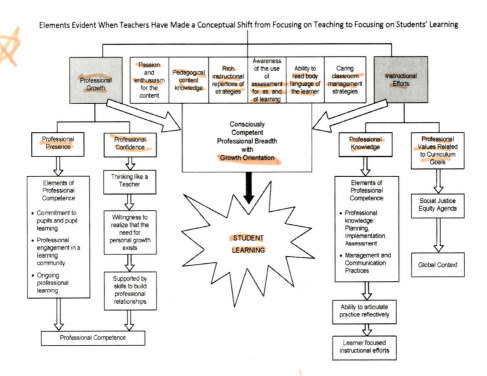

Elements Evident When Teachers Have Made a Conceptual Shift from Focusing on Teaching to Focusing on Students' Learning

It may be to your advantage to use these concepts to describe yourself and your capabilities as you address various questions in your interview. This diagram represents Professional Shift Theory (*pst*). As this diagram shows, always keep the focus of your answers on providing evidence that you can and will support students' learning. For further information about this diagram and *pst* theory read Maynes & Hatt, 2012.

CHAPTER 8

ANTICIPATE THE QUESTIONS

Chapters 8, 9 and 10 of this book will focus on how to address the questions that are asked of you in an interview. You should, however, first notice one critical thing. The last seven chapters have been devoted to what you do to prepare for the interview before that first question is ever posed. Being well prepared by anticipating what an interview is all about will help you be better prepared for the brief face-to-face time you will have with your interviewers.

In reality, the questions you will be asked in an interview will be as varied as the people who may be interviewing you. Questions will be influenced by the type of job being offered, the time of year of the interview, the people on the interview team, the philosophy of education that predominates in the school jurisdiction, the panel (elementary or secondary), the mission of the school, and any current local issues that may bring attention to teacher qualifications and skills (e.g., religious views, bullying, extra-curricular activities, etc.). The only way you can really know what questions you will be asked is to speak directly to the person who was interviewed immediately before you, and that is unlikely to happen!

The best way for you to prepare for specific questions is to think more broadly about the types of questions you are likely to be asked. Ask yourself, "What is the range of responsibilities of the advertised position?" You can narrow down this range of responsibilities by thinking about whom you are likely to influence and interact with during your time in the role. This group is likely to include, in proportionate order, students, teacher colleagues, the school principal, parents, community members, and other teachers outside of your school.

Once you have identified this list of people you are likely to influence in this role, ask yourself another question. "What interactions am I likely to have with each of these groups?" This will help you to identify skills and knowledge that might relate to each type of interaction with each group. An example of a way to organize your thoughts about this is provided.

Groups of People I Will Interact With	Type of Interactions I will Likely Have with Each Group of People
Students	• plan for instruction • determine gaps or areas for growth • read and understand goals of the local curriculum guidelines • teach; direct learning • assess progress with learning • provide feedback and direction for growth • conference about learning with students and parents • arrange additional supports for learning as needed • teach social skills as needed
Teacher Colleagues	• cooperate in achieving the goals of the school • work together to support the desired school climate • support each other's professional growth • share resources • mentor growth of new teachers

School Principal	<ul><li>report students' progress, and their special learning and social needs</li><li>cooperate in achieving the goals of the school</li><li>identify resource needs for your program</li><li>assist with the development and communication of the school's mission</li><li>teach effectively</li><li>manage classroom and school wide behavior to optimize learning</li></ul>
Parents	<ul><li>identify program direction and goals</li><li>monitor and report each student's academic and social progress</li><li>provide examples of student's work and share information about both criteria and standards for achievement</li><li>engage parents in significant and appropriate decisions</li></ul>
Community Members	<ul><li>advance the goals of the school</li><li>teach students citizenship concepts</li><li>engage students in community projects</li></ul>
Other Colleagues Outside of the School	<ul><li>advance the goals of the school jurisdiction</li><li>support the growth goals of the jurisdiction for individual teachers</li><li>participate cooperatively in the professional community of learners and the political organization(s) that form your union/federation</li></ul>

This list can help you consider the sources and foci of questions you are likely to face in an interview.

Teachers in the profession are also evaluated regularly. Their evaluations are based on shared criteria that are known to the teachers and are widely used to develop individual goals for professional growth. In some jurisdictions, these same criteria are used to evaluate the development of skills in teacher preparation programs in Faculties of Education.

To help you prepare for teaching interviews in your jurisdiction, you should investigate the teacher and teacher candidate evaluation criteria used in your area. These will usually be available through school board web sites and through local teacher union connections. In the example that follows, the criteria used in the province of Ontario and the local teacher's federations are used to illustrate.

In Ontario, there are five key areas of teacher influence that are the foci of teacher's responsibilities. While these names of categories are specific to Ontario, the breadth of the categories is applicable across jurisdictions. These categories include:

- Commitment to pupils and pupil learning;
- Leadership and community;
- Ongoing professional learning;
- Professional knowledge, including planning, implementing, and assessing; and
- Management and communication practices.

Before your interview, find out what key areas are addressed in teachers' performance appraisals in your area. Each of these key areas of influence can be expanded to provide more direction about what is expected of teachers in their professional roles. These areas of influence can then provide a source of questions for teacher interviews. A breakdown of these criteria might yield a set of specifics such as the following:

Commitment to pupils and pupil learning, including:

- shows care and commitment to pupils
- shows commitment to teaching

- treats pupils equitably and with respect
- creates learning opportunities for problem solving, critical thinking, and decision making
- adjusts teaching and learning strategies to support all learners, including identified learners (e.g., ELL, identified special needs, etc.)

Leadership and communities, including:

- collaborates with others to create a learning community
- assumes professional responsibilities (e.g., planning, instruction, assessment, supervision of learning, etc.)

Ongoing professional learning, including:

- demonstrates commitment to professional growth
- engages in reflection to improve instruction
- contributes positively to the community of learnership in the classroom, school, and board

Professional knowledge (e.g., planning, implementing, assessing), including:

- identifies lesson expectations, including learning goals and learning skills
- understands and identifies curriculum content, including facts, concepts, and skills
- uses assessment that aligns with learning expectations; *for, as,* and *of* learning
- describes pre-assessment of learners including prior knowledge, modification, accommodations, and alternative expectations for learning based on identification of special needs
- plans an effective learning environment and related resources
- plans and develops effective teaching and learning strategies
- plans for practice and consolidation of learning

- plans for application of learning in real contexts that require problem solving and complex thinking and decision making
- connects new learning to prior learning through an introduction that surfaces prior knowledge
- uses strategies that engage learners, support learning, and encourage learning progress
- uses technology and resources appropriately to support learning
- uses assessment strategies and recording devices that support plans for new learning
- engages students in strategies that assess *for, as,* and *of* learning (e.g, diagnostic, formative, and summative)
- times and paces lessons to support students' learning success

Management and communication practices, including:

- models effective oral and written communications
- demonstrates effective use of appropriate electronic communications
- uses effective questioning techniques to support learning
- promotes a positive and collaborative learning environment
- uses proactive classroom management techniques to support a positive learning environment
- uses appropriate management techniques to redirect learners as needed
- reinforces positive, productive learning and social behaviours
- promotes citizenship and social justice concepts in the classroom and school

Each one of these five areas of teacher responsibility can be used to generate questions for teacher hiring. While it is likely that teacher hiring teams are not as systematic as this in developing the questions for a hiring interview, it is certain that their questions will encompass these basic teacher competencies because they define the role of a teacher.

To provide examples of how interview teams might use this list of teacher competencies to generate appropriate performance based questions for a set of interviews, some samples related to each area are provided below.

Examples

Commitment to Pupils and Pupil Learning

Explain what we would see in a visit to your classroom that would demonstrate to us that you are engaging, challenging, and supporting the students you teach.

Leadership and Community

Tell us about a time when you provided leadership and contributed to the community of learnership in your chosen profession.

Ongoing Professional Learning

Tell us about a time when you worked with other professionals to support each other's learning about effective teaching.

Professional Knowledge

Tell us about a time when you used your professional knowledge to plan, support, and assess students' learning effectively.

Management and Communication Practices

Tell us about a time when you had a conflict with a student who was unmotivated to learn and how you addressed this situation with both the student and the parents.

What is being asked? What is really being asked?

If you look at any one of these questions as they are presented, they seem simplistic and very easy to answer. They seem to direct you to just tell a story. However, you always need to ask yourself, with every question in an interview, "What is the question?" and "What is the real question?" or "What is being asked?" and "What is really being asked?"

For example, consider the question:

Tell us about a time when you had a conflict with a student who was unmotivated to learn and how you addressed this situation with both the student and the parents.

This question is trying to give interviewers an opportunity to determine if you have the following knowledge and skills:

- Can you articulate a situation clearly?
- Can you consider alternative perspectives in a situation?
- Can you create a positive resolution to a conflict?
- Can you manage a conflict while maintaining the best interests of the student as your focus?
- Can you involve students in understanding the relationships between actions and consequences?
- Can you communicate with parents in a positive partnership to support students' growth?
- Can you reflect on your professional practice to support productive action in similar situations in the future?

In order to address each of these aspects of your practice in your interview response, you need to go beyond what was asked in the question to answer what the real question is about. To do this, think broadly about the area of professional practice that is being addressed in each question. Once you determine which of the five areas of practice the question fits, structure your answer as outlined in previous chapters.

For example, tell the interviewers what structure you will follow in your answer. Then, tell the story, being sure to protect confidentiality of participants. Then, move from the specific to the general. That is, explain to the interviewers that this story is an example of how you would address a class of responsibilities (e.g., how you would address all management and communication tasks in your teaching role). Finally, explain what you might do differently to improve the outcome and further support students' learning (remember to always keep that as your focus), and close the response by telling the interviewers what you have said in your answer by reviewing the parts of the response.

If you address every interview question in this fashion consistently, you will be sure to answer questions thoroughly and include examples that highlight your professional skills while addressing the needs of the employers. Also, if you have this structure for responses in mind as you engage in an interview, you will be able to display the maturity of your understanding of the role while convincing the interviewers that you have enough experience to address their needs for well qualified, confident teachers.

The following chapter will give you several examples of how to structure interview question responses and provide some sample questions to help you practise this skill.

CHAPTER 9

STRUCTURE YOUR RESPONSES

In a competitive teaching market, your ability to stand out in an interview is critical if you want to teach. If your resume and accompanying documentation have been prepared carefully and you have additional skills beyond the most basic teacher qualifications, you may be invited to an interview. This is your time to shine, but you can only do that if your answers to interview questions also stand out. Both content and structure will help you to do that in every answer.

In previous chapters, you learned about how to apply for a teaching position, how to organize the essential paper work to support your application, how to make your resume really draw the attention of employers, how to understand the perspectives of potential interviewers, how to make a strong first impression, how to think about the questions that are asked, and how to anticipate what those questions are most likely to address.

In this chapter, you will have an opportunity to learn more about how to structure answers to questions and have some practice in doing that by following the case studies of both strong and weaker responses to spot things that should be improved to strengthen the responses.

You have learned from earlier chapters that all interview questions may not be strong questions because of the way interview teams may be prepared and formed. However, even if weak questions are asked of you in an interview, you can still impress interviewers by answering these questions with a strong structure that tells them more than they asked for in the exemplary answer you provide.

Working with What you are Given

Some years ago I had a newly certified teacher contact me before his interview for a full time teaching job. I had provided a two-hour workshop for his cohort of graduating teachers about interviews and how they operate. He had contacted me for a refresher discussion just before his interview. We talked a lot about question frameworks during our discussions. He was completely taken aback in his interview because of the nature of the questions he was asked. He had the presence of mind to record these questions right after the interview so he could think about them and perhaps use them to prepare for future interviews.

These are the questions he was asked:

Tell us a little bit about yourself.

What is your idea of balanced literacy?

How would you handle conflicts with a parent?

How would you handle conflicts with principals? How would you handle issues if a principal has issues with your teaching practices?

Talk about your experience integrating Smart technology into the classroom.

What does a Catholic School look like?

How would you model your faith outside the classroom in the community?

How would your students describe you?

How would your Associate Teachers describe you?

Explain what formative assessments and summative assessments are like?

If you received a bunch of tests and all the students performed poorly, what would you do?

What would you do if a student finished their work early?

This province has provincial standardized tests. How would you prepare?

Have you worked with students with special needs?

As you read through this array of questions and the sheer volume of them, you will realize a few things. First, this is a separate school system interview. Second, there are many questions here . . . 14 of them . . . meaning one of two things. Either this interview was a very long one or the interviewer expected very brief answers to the questions. Third, you can see from the questions that they were likely compiled by one person with little or no interview training. Here are some clues to support that conclusion:

- the final question is poorly worded, inviting a yes or no answer;
- there are two questions about conflict; in a well structured interview, one should tell the interviewers all they would need to know about your framework for handing conflicts;
- some wording seems to misdirect the interviewee or create a tone that is out of phase with the usual tone of an interview ("Tell us a bit . . ." . . . . are they saying be very brief with this part? And ". . . you received a bunch of tests . . ." . . . It's unclear whether these are tests the teacher set and the word "bunch" seems oddly casual in the context of an interview.)

Finally, the questions seem to have been brainstormed but left unfiltered or unedited after the brainstorming stage. As you can see from the order of questions on the list, when the interviewer thought of one question about a topic, this generated further ideas about the same topic. For example, there are two questions about faith, two about conflict, and three about assessment. A well prepared interviewer would form one substantial question about each of these areas and allow the interviewee to frame an answer without clues to the response they want built into the answer. One question ("How would you handle conflicts with a parent? How would you handle conflicts with principals? How would you handle issues if a principal has issues with your teaching practices?") seems to be focused on two aspects of professional practice. It first asks about management skills related to handing conflict, and then it relates this to professional development to improve your teaching. This would be a very difficult question to respond to because it calls for two different starting points in the response.

Also, some questions do not provide any reasonable focus for the interviewee. For example, the question "What would you do if a student finished their work early?" could be looking for a simple list of possible tasks students could do or may be inviting an interviewee to speak about tracking and documenting the need for gifted programming for a student. I would suspect that the interviewer would be a little puzzled by the range of responses this question would elicit.

To find some meaning in this range of questions, sort them into the five categories that you learned about in Chapter 8. Use an organizer such as the one provided below:

Commitment to Pupils and Pupil Learning	Leadership and Community	Ongoing Professional Learning	Professional Knowledge (including planning, implementing, and assessing)	Management and Communication Practices

Now, check your sorted questions against the lists that are provided. Think about why you may have sorted a question into one category if you placed it differently than we did. What slants or perspectives on the question might we have viewed differently?

- **Commitment to pupils and pupil learning**
  Tell us a little bit about yourself.
  How would your students describe you?
  How would your Associate Teachers describe you?

- **Leadership and community**
  What does a Catholic School look like?
  How would you model your faith outside the classroom in the community?

- **Ongoing professional learning**
  How would you handle issues if a principal has issues with your teaching practices?

- **Professional knowledge, including planning, implementing, and assessing**
  What is your idea of balanced literacy?
  Talk about your experience integrating Smart technology into the classroom.
  Explain what formative assessments and summative assessments are like.
  If you received a bunch of tests and all the students performed poorly, what would you do?
  What would you do if a student finished their work early?
  This province has provincial standardized tests. How would you prepare?
  Have you worked with students with special needs?

- **Management and communication practices**
  How would you handle conflicts with a parent?
  How would you handle conflicts with principals?

Which questions did you put into a different category? Consider why. Your sorting is not wrong. Any differences simply point out that the questions are so unclear as to elicit totally different interpretations from different people. This makes conducting a fair set of interviews very difficult.

As you can see from this sorting exercise, the majority of these questions focused on the aspect of the interviewee's professional knowledge. A well-organized interview will attempt to address all five of these areas of professional identity with well-crafted questions for each area. If questions are well crafted, they will provide the interviewee enough scope to include specific examples that will provide evidence of the range of their skills.

As you prepare your resume for a teaching job application, it is wise to examine your qualifications, as you present them in these documents, against these five headings. This will help you prepare examples for your interview and may help you focus professional growth on areas that seem to be weaker or underrepresented. As you address gaps in your own resume, you can manage your longer-term growth plan for professional development.

Anticipation is the Key to Success

Regardless of the interviewers' skills in crafting and asking interview questions, there are some things you can anticipate to help you prepare for all aspects of the possible strong or weaker questions you may be asked.

First, you can predict the focus of questions. These will be based on what is most expected of you as a teacher. So, there will always be questions that focus on the following general themes:

- instruction;
- assessment;
- differentiation;
- conflict;
- communication;
- classroom management; and
- professional growth.

These questions are totally predictable because, as any experienced principal will tell you, if a new teacher is struggling with their job, the problems they are having will relate to one or more of these areas of their role. Principals therefore are sensitive to these areas because they will take up a great deal of administrative time and skill to address any weaknesses in these areas, once the teacher has started into the profession.

Second, you can always sort (in your "on the spot" thinking) each of these themes in the questions into one of the five categories of professional performance. This will help you structure your response. For example, if the question is about conflict, you could start your response by saying, "*Good management and communication are essential characteristics in my classroom. So, to address this type of conflict I always . . . .*" By starting your response like this, you have made the listeners aware of your professional framework and taken a specific example of conflict that is in the question to a higher level, of an issue related to management and communication, which then allows you to come back to this as a general summary for your answer. Note the use of the active voice in the response. Even if the question asks you to identify what you would do (e.g., in the future), always answer in the present (e.g., "are"). This helps you to project more confidence.

Third, be on the lookout for "hot topic" questions. These are questions that will relate to local issues that are either financially sensitive or media sensitive. Following, there are two extreme examples to illustrate.

Example 1

If your area has recently had a violent incident take place in a school (e.g., a suicide, a physical conflict that resulted in an injury to a teacher or a student, a shooting or stabbing, or a road or bus accident), you are very likely to get an interview question that relates to safety in the schools.

Example 2

If your area has recently been the focus of media attention related to a financial scandal in a school (e.g., a teacher misusing funds collected for an event), you are very likely to get a question about security and image of teachers in the community.

It makes good sense that interview foci will reflect current high profile concerns in the community because these will be uppermost in people's minds. You can make yourself aware of this type of local issue by talking to teachers and other members of the community, reading local media, or by reading the minutes of local school board meetings. As well, the school's web site is likely to give you many ideas about what the school sees as its current issues and concerns. You should be well aware of the school site before your interview.

STARR Format for Answering Interview Questions

In Chapter 7, examples of how to structure interview responses were given. Three aspects of your responses should include: Tell them what you're going to do; Do it; Tell them what you did. However, nerves are a factor when applicants face an interview. Sometimes, if a person is very nervous, they will tend to forget details of preparation for an interview and plans to organize responses in a certain way may be neglected.

Some interviewees may find it easier to remember to structure their responses if they learn an acronym for the parts of the response. One acronym that is commonly used to structure answers in an interview is called STARR. This is a five-part interview answering system that would also work well with teaching interview questions. The parts of the **STARR** acronym remind you to include:

S = SITUATION

Describe the situation or issue.

T = TASK

Describe what needed to be done.

A = ACTION

Describe the action you took.

R = RESULTS

Describe the positive and negative outcomes; include what you learned and what you would do differently next time.

R = RELEVENCE

Describe how this situation is related to this job application.

> *Note:* Sometimes this approach is referred to as STAR, which includes the first four of the five steps outlined above. STARR is more appropriate for a performance-based interview style since employers will be very interested in hearing how you will address comparable situations in the future (e.g., describing the relevance of what you learned).

If you prefer the STARR (or STAR) approach to answering interview questions, you may find it useful to visit some online sites that will expand on these steps. Some useful STAR sites include:

- *http://www.youtube.com/watch?v=A95xTOGQ17A*
  This site provides some useful direction about how to answer an interview question such as, "Tell us about yourself as a teacher". It reminds viewers to consider what is important and what is relevant as you address this question and not to get carried away by including overly personal or overly detailed information that does not relate to the job you are seeking.

- *http://www.guukle.com/star-interview-questions/*
  This commercial site will provide a long list of questions (100 of them!) that relate to job interviews. They are worded as performance based (or competency based) questions and they may provide you some extra exposure to that type of questioning format.

- *www.interview-skills.co.uk/competency-based-interviews-STAR.aspx*
  This commercial site will provide further details about the STAR approach to answering interview questions.

However, when you visit these sites, be aware of two key things. First, these are mostly commercial sites. They are trying to sell you the training they want to provide. Just be aware that the training is more geared to business interviews than to teaching interviews and they are very different. Second, some online sites will try to convince you that there is a limited set of interview questions that you can somehow come to know. There isn't. The interview questions you may face are as varied as the people, places, times, circumstances, issues, values, and job market that you face. You will be better prepared for an interview if you have a framework for the job you want and mentally slot the questions you face into that framework. You can be certain that the framework will be the same for the role in virtually any circumstance even though you can be equally as certain that the questions will be different.

Telling Your Story to Sell Your Skills

Because you can anticipate the main topics of interview questions and you have a framework for responding to each one, you can prepare your stories ahead of time. This will help you feel more relaxed and confident in the interview.

In the STARR answer format the first two steps of your response require that you explain the situation (S= situation), then describe what needed to be done (T=Task). Before your interview, prepare a story of the situation and task for each of the categories of questions that are outlined in the section "Anticipation is the key to success", earlier in this chapter.

By anticipating the need for these contextualized stories, you can help your responses to flow more smoothly and impress interviewers with the details you can retrieve from memory quickly to illustrate your strengths in key areas.

Assessment as an Interview Skill

Responding well to an interview question is about thorough assessment. This includes three types of assessment that you must be well prepared to examine on the spot as questions are asked in the interview.

1. **Self-assessment**—Know why you are the perfect candidate for this teaching job and be prepared to articulate that in the first few minutes of your interview.

2. **Interviewer assessment**—Know what perspectives, backgrounds, and interview training your interviewers have brought to this task. This will help you reframe their questions so that you can make the most of them as vehicles for displaying what you bring to the job.

3. **Question assessment**—If you consider each question as a sub-set of possible questions that could be asked about any one of the five areas of teacher preparation that have been outlined in this chapter, you will be able to provide a contextualized opening to your responses that will give them structure and allow you the broadest possible scope for your answers.

So, remember that knowing possible questions that may be used in an interview may be useful in helping you prepare, but knowing how to use a response framework will help you stand out from among other job applicants.

CHAPTER 10

TAKE CONTROL OF THE CLOSING OF YOUR INTERVIEW

By the time you get to the end of your teaching interview you will be drained emotionally and physically. Even though you have only been in the interview for about 20 minutes so far, you have spent days preparing and you are heavily invested in this high stakes opportunity. However, you still have a few things working in your favour. One of these things is your interview team. Remember that they want you to succeed. They remember the anxiety of their first interviews and some may have been interviewed recently for other roles in teaching. They will be empathetic to your position but you will need to remember as well that they are looking for the 'best of the best' as they prepare to hire a teacher. Use the final minutes of the interview to convince them that this is you!

The second major thing that will work in your favour is a strong closing to your interview. A strong closing will make your exit from the interview memorable and will help interviewers consolidate their overall impression of you. You want to leave your interview with interviewers being confident in the honesty and integrity of your answers and a strong closing can help you create that impression.

To prepare for a strong closing for your interview, remember that an interview has an hourglass shape. That is, the interview has an open-ended question at the beginning and an open-ended question at the end but is more structured in the middle. To review, the open ended question at the beginning of an interview is often a variation of, "Tell us about yourself (as a teacher)". It may have more personalized wording such as "Tell us what we will see when we visit your classroom" or "Tell us what your students would say about you as a teacher". With any of these variants, the focus is the same. They are asking about your professional beliefs and practices in a way that gives them a first opportunity to measure your confidence and poise as you answer.

 However, the open-ended question at the end of the interview is likely to be one of two types. It could include a question that asks you to explain your weaknesses or it could be even more open by asking you if you have any questions for the interview committee. The interviewers may start this part of your interview with a prelude that may over- relax you as the interview closes. Be cautious! This is an extremely important part of the interview because it is the last impression you will leave with the interview team. Last impressions may be even more important than first impressions, especially if your interview is one of the first in a long list of applicants. By planning well, you can leave your interviewers with something very positive to help them remember you.

If the interviewers are going to leave the end of your interview totally open, they may start this last segment with a prelude comment such, "We have asked you several questions. Now it's your turn. Do you have any questions for us?" Sounds inviting doesn't it?

This is where many teacher applicants undermine the strong impression they have made on the interview team in the earlier parts of their interview. The advice we are about to give you will seem counter-intuitive but please listen carefully. Do **not** ask a question at this point. It is counter-intuitive to think this way because your potential employers have just invited you to do this. So, let's consider why we are giving you this advice.

What questions could you reasonably ask at this point? Since you likely don't know the members of your interview team and have only minimal information about their backgrounds, you can't ask specific questions about their interests. Even if you could, those questions are unlikely to be really relevant to *your* job application. Also, if you ask a question about some mechanical aspect of the job, such a when they will make their decision about your application, this has the effect of figuratively pushing your committee into a corner of being unsure how to answer the question. When you start seeing your interviewers looking at each other, you will know they are feeling pushed. This is something you want to avoid. You don't want to be remembered as the job candidate who made them feel uncomfortable.

Another common mistake made at this point of the interview is for applicants to ask a dead end question. A dead end question is one that interviewers will answer with a "yes" or a "no" response. A common example of a dead end question in teaching interviews is, "Will there be an opportunity for me to volunteer to run extra-curricular activities in this job?" This is a dead end question because the obvious answer is "yes" . . . not much of a conversation starter is it?

You want this part of your interview to be as well structured, dynamic and memorable as the rest of your interview. To take control of this aspect of the interview and really make your interviewers sit up and take notice of your confidence and your preparation, say "no" when you are asked if you have any questions. BUT, don't leave the "no" hanging. Here's what to do instead.

As soon as you hear the preamble to the last question, you will know if you will be invited to ask a question before you leave the interview. However, now that you know that you're about to say "no", be sure you are ready to follow it up with the summative statement that will make you memorable. Here is an example of a closing statement you might use or adjust to your personal style.

No, I don't have any questions right now but I would like to close this interview by saying that I have enjoyed this opportunity to show why I am the ideal candidate for this position. I have demonstrated through my answers that I have the qualifications, professional skills, leadership and teamwork qualities, commitment to professional growth, and the management and communication skills to make me a highly effective teacher with your school (or board) team. I look forward to working with you as part of your school (or board) community.

Why is a Good Interview Closing Important?

What makes this an effective interview closing? It does several things for you. It says that you have thought ahead to plan for the ending of your interview. It says you are confident in what you have to offer an employer. It revisits the question framework you have used throughout your interview to structure responses. It demonstrates your positive attitude and confident tone, both of which employers want parents to see in teachers. Finally, it puts a clear and concise ending on your interview so that everyone is confortable that you are finished. And, you did all of that in just three short but well planned sentences!

There are, of course, other equally effective ways you can end an interview when you are asked if you have any questions. Here are two more examples. You could say something along the lines of either of the following:

No, I don't have any questions at the moment, but I would like to close this interview by reminding you that I bring four valuable teacher characteristics to this position. I am firm, fair, fun, and flexible . . . .the four f's of good teaching. My students will see me as firm because they will know that our classroom is a place dedicated to learning and to supporting each person's progress. They will see me as fair because we will have a well established set of classroom routines that will help optimize learning time and a set of classroom rules that will help us create a classroom that is respectful of differences. They will see me as fun because I will create active, engaging, challenging, and differentiated learning opportunities for each student. They will see me as flexible because they will know that their interests and talents will have a place in our learning and that they will be supported in reaching their own successes. By being firm, fair, fun, and flexible, I can be sure to create the kind of learning environment where every one of my students can thrive.

Consider this closing statement compared to the previous example. Which one do you prefer? Why? What does this second example do for you as a closing message to interviewers? Look at how specific key words are used to identify your commitment to strong teaching. Words and phrases such as "dedicated to learning", "optimize learning time", "support each person's progress", "respectful of differences", "active, engaging, challenging, and differentiated" are strong messages to leave as you get ready to end your time with the interviewers. This is the time to make every word count.

Here is another example of a powerful interview closing that will leave that positive and confident impression you want.

No, I do not have any questions at the moment, but I would like to close this interview by saying that we know that the best predictor of future performance in a job is past performance in that job. To support my application for this position I have provided XX examples of practice teaching reports that show that my past performance as a teacher has been exemplary. I am able to design and maintain a classroom learning environment that is productive, challenging, engaging, and differentiated. My classroom will have these features because I will use my abilities to ensure that every child has optimal support for their learning. I will ensure that my professional practice is always current so that I can use the most effective strategies, technology, and assessment approaches to ensure the success of every child. My past performance as a teacher is what I know will be my future performance, and it will be enriched even more by on the job experience.

Once again, compare this closing to the previous two examples. Look for key words and phrases in each example that create the strongly positive and confident tone you want to leave.

You may find that you have better ideas for this part of your interview. Try writing your own closing statement that responds to the offer to ask a closing question. Have colleagues help you assess the closing to be sure it is leaving all of the interconnected messages that you want to have as your lasting impression for this interview team.

What if they don't ask you if you have any questions?

Your interview team may decide not to provide you with a time to ask any questions at the end of your interview. They may instead give you a further question that is designed to examine your strategies for self-improvement and professional reflection. They may instead ask a question that might serve as a kind of confidence trap unless you prepare for it ahead of time.

This type of closing question may be framed as some variation of the following.

What would you say is your biggest weakness?

This can be a very scary question if you try to tackle it without preparation, so be sure to consider this as one possibility before your interview. This question can throw you off guard because your whole interview so far has been about your strengths and your suitability for this job. Now, a potentially negative tone is being introduced, and that's not the final impression you want to leave in your interview.

Just as you did previously with "crystal ball" style questions, you need to reframe this question. You still need to talk about a weakness but frame the answer so that you preface the weakness with a statement of strength and end the statement with a comment about how you try to correct or improve on this weakness. State the weakness in the most positive terms possible. Here are a couple of examples of how you could do that. Even better, chose to identify a weakness that many people will consider to be a strength.

Example 1

> *I am a very energetic person but that level of energy can be difficult for other people. I try to buffer my energy level by being aware of other people's learning styles and I try to incorporate their way of working into how I work with them. This approach has helped me to be successful in many cooperative efforts and seems to work well with other people.*

If we analyze this example, we can see the weakness, the high energy level, might be considered a strength by an employer. That makes it a good example to use because they will see that you may work harder with so much energy. You have also bookended you weakness by stating it as a strength at the beginning of your statement and by showing how you try to manage your energy level to make it advantageous for you in the workplace.

Example 2

> *I have advanced skills with computer technology and online learning. This can be a concern because it may be intimidating for some colleagues whose computer skills are developing. I try to bridge any problems with this by offering support to my colleagues and by engaging in shared cross-classroom projects so that colleagues can support students' learning with their specialized skills in art or physical education while I support our shared group of learners with my technology skills. By doing this, I learn new skills from my colleagues and they learn new skills from me, and our students benefit from both sets of skills.*

Notice in this example how you very carefully word any comparison of other colleagues. Their skills are "developing", not "weak". Always bring the advantage of your solution to this strength back to the ability to support better student learning when you can.

Practising Your Interview Closing

Practise trying to frame some sample interview endings that address the question, "*What would you say is your biggest weakness?*" Use the examples of strengths listed below to try to present these as weaknesses bookended by strengths and solutions. Compare your responses to those of other teacher candidates to get some perspective on how each one is likely to be perceived by interviewers.

Samples to address in your interview closing:

- breadth of work experience before teaching
- previous intense work with a severely disabled child
- work experience as an educational assistant
- artistic abilities
- previous experience on sports teams at an advanced level

If you close your interview in a strong way, you will leave the impression that you want to leave with your interviewers. The interview closing is often the most poorly prepared part of an interview. However, it is not a part of your interview you want to neglect if you intend to leave a favourable impression.

Using Your Professional Portfolio in your Interview

Professional portfolios are valued differently in different jurisdictions. You have probably spent a great deal of time and effort developing your portfolio and it probably provides a considerable amount of evidence that you have certain desirable teaching skills. Some jurisdictions will indicate on their web site what they expect you to provide with your application. This may include submitting a professional teaching portfolio. Increasingly, school boards who want to see your professional portfolio ask to have it submitted in electronic format. Follow the specific directions of each jurisdiction very closely.

If the board where you have an interview does not require the submission of a professional teaching portfolio with your online application, you have the option to bring your portfolio to your interview.

If you do decide to bring your portfolio to an interview, be prepared to use it strategically. A portfolio has one purpose. It provides **concrete evidence** that you have certain professional qualifications and skills. If this evidence is to have value in your interview, you will have to use the portfolio to show this evidence when it is appropriate to do so.

You also need to be aware that interviewers will not welcome you taking time away from their pre-determined interview plan to use your portfolio inefficiently. Following are some suggestions for how to make effective use of your portfolio to support the verbal evidence you use in your interview.

- Take your portfolio with you to every interview. Have the portfolio fully developed and be sure that there is a professional looking cover and spine on your portfolio. Carry it in your left hand to leave your right hand free for shaking if the interviewers invite this at the outset of your interview.

- As you settle into the interview chair, place your portfolio to your right (the position of privilege) with the spine facing the interviewers. Even if you never use the portfolio during your interview, the interviewers will be aware that you've come prepared for the possibility and that your professional work looks polished and impressive.

- Mark key places in your portfolio that may be the focus of anticipated interview topics (e.g., an example of a differentiation strategy, a unit plan you've designed, a web quest you've designed, etc.). Be sure that you know exactly where to find each piece of evidence very quickly when it is relevant. It will not work in your favour if interviewers perceive that you are wasting precious interview time to find the appropriate documents.

- At the end of your interview you have the option of offering to leave your portfolio with the interview committee so they can review it. It is likely that they will not want to do this because they may not have time and they may not want to take responsibility for the security of the document. However, the offer could be made.

- You may also want to present copies of a specific useful part of your portfolio to members of the interview team. If you choose to do this, do it carefully. Only provide photocopies of items that are truly outstanding. Good examples might be a unit plan that shows a combined grade integrated unit plan for a new curriculum guideline, a boldly coloured web quest assignment, a copy of the screen shots of a well developed SMARTboard lesson component, or other components that will impress the interviewers with your skills. The interview team will not want copies of your qualifications or your resume. They already have access to those documents. Do not share copies of anything that you do not want others to use. If you've provided amazing copies of a useful and classroom-ready product, some principals will have this in the hands of their teachers the next day. Have your name on the things you share this way. Make such a presentation part of your closing comments as you leave the interview and invite interviewers to share your materials with other teachers. This leaves a good impression about your collegial attitude.

How you use your portfolio in your interview is your decision. However, it is always wise to read the tone and body language of your interviewers, to get a sense of how they will perceive time viewing your portfolio, before you consult it during your interview time.

Leaving the Interview

The focus of this chapter has been on taking control of the ending of your interview. Since every interview team will end their time with applicants in slightly different ways, there may be other approaches that you will encounter when you are signaled that your interview is almost over. However, if you prepare for the two possibilities outlined in this chapter, and you remember that virtually all interviews have an hourglass shape, you can consider preparing a short statement for the end of the interview that does the one thing you want it to do . . . leave the impression of confidence and control!

CHAPTER 11

PUTTING YOUR FIRST INTERVIEW EXPERIENCE TO GOOD USE

Reviewing what you Have Learned about Interviews

In the previous chapters of this book you have learned a number of things that should make you both optimistic about your prospects for securing your first full time teaching job, and the way to strengthen your interview skills to achieve that outcome.

You have learned that the coming years will see a huge window of openings in the teaching profession across Canada. You are now aware of how to apply for a teaching position in Canada and resources that may help secure an international position if that is your choice. You have learned about the importance of developing the paper work that will be required to support the application you will forward to the school jurisdictions of your choice.

You have learned about how to make the best first impression in an interview by dressing for the role you want. Ways to identify who will interview and what perspectives each person is likely to bring to their decisions about hiring were reviewed.

You have learned how to read the interviewer's intentions as your interview starts and how to understand the body language message that will transmit their expectations at the beginning of your interview.

You have also learned that all these ideas are very important considerations before you actually get to address the interview questions. To prepare for the types of questions you are likely to hear in interviews, you have learned about the style of interview questions that are possible. You have learned about how to analyze and address questions using a framework that sorts each question related to various teacher competencies. You have learned how to anticipate the focus of questions that you will be asked based on the interests of interviewers in finding the right fit for their position.

Finally, you have learned how to structure responses to each question to impress interviewers with your organization and insights. You have reviewed options for how to address the closing of your interview in order to leave a strong impression.

In this final chapter, you will learn how to learn from your interview.

After the Questions Are Finished, What's Next?

The person who has lead your interview will likely be a school principal who is acting either on behalf of the school board (hiring for a system position) or on behalf of an individual school (hiring for a school-based position). It is usual for the leader of the team to make some closing comments for the interviewers after you have finished with your closing answers.

The nature of the closing comments made by the lead interviewer will vary, depending on the nature of the position, and the decisions that have been made locally about hiring practices. These comments may include any of the following:

- thanking you for attending this interview;
- giving information about the expected timelines for decisions about hires from this round of interviewing;
- reviewing the position parameters and explaining the process used to select people for later hiring (i.e., this is often referred to a "pool"); and
- explaining how hires will be notified of the results of their interview.

When you are finished your interview and leave the room, make written records of each of the messages about these items that you are given at the end of your interview.

Reflection After an Interview

Once you have left your interview, it is wise to write down the questions you can remember from the interview as soon as you can. Try to get the wording as close as possible to the exact way these questions were asked. Below each question you have recalled, make some jot notes about the key things you included in your response.

If your first interview was unsuccessful, the practice of reflecting on recent interviews will help you to strengthen your preparation for the next interview. As you examine the interview questions that you have recalled, consider the following ideas:

- What opening comments were made to welcome me to the interview and give structure to the interview time before the formal questioning started?
- Were the questions asked as "crystal ball questions" or as performance- (or competency) based questions?
- How many questions were asked?
- What was the opening question that was asked?
- Did one interviewer ask all of the questions or were they distributed among the interview team?
- Were you able to manage good eye contact with interview team members during the interview regardless of who was asking the questions?
- Were you able to structure responses to your interview questions as you had planned before the interview?
- If you had an assortment of structures in the interview questions you were asked, (i.e., some "crystal ball" and some performance-based), were you successful at restructuring the questions to a performance-based question before you started your response? If not, why?
- Did the interview team seem to be working from a list of criteria (or look-fors) as they listened to your responses?

- Which topics that were part of the questions did you expect to address in your interview?
- Which topics that were part of the questions in your interview were a surprise/ unexpected?
- How did you feel about your interview as a whole, immediately after your interview?
- Did your interview results (i.e., whether you were offered the job) match your impression of the interview? If they did not match, what factors may have caused your impressions to be different than the outcome?
- What did you say to maintain your professional composure and your integrity when you received the disappointing phone call to communicate negative results about your interview?
- List three things you wished you had done differently in your interview.

To this extensive list of ideas to help you review your interview performance, add your own reflection questions. Even if your interview was a success and you were offered the job, you may soon face other interviews for advancement purposes or for new specialized teaching opportunities within the board. Teaching yourself about your interview strengths and areas for growth will help you make the best use of your interview preparation to help you present yourself in the best possible light during the next interview.

Requesting a Debriefing after your Interview

One of the closing comments that may be made by the lead interviewer will include a description of the debriefing opportunity you may have after your interview. Debriefing is a valuable process to invest time in if you have been unsuccessful in an interview, but not all boards use debriefing as part of their interview sequence. Before your interview, you may want to ask local principals how they feel about debriefing candidates and how they are likely to feel if an unsuccessful candidate asked for this opportunity.

It is usual at the end of an interview for the lead interviewer to collect, and later destroy, all written records made by the interviewers. This is done to protect the privacy of individuals. So, if you are interested in a debriefing you should ask for this shortly after being notified about the results of the interview. If the person conducting the debriefing has no written records of your interview, the debriefing experience is unlikely to be of much value to you. In many jurisdictions, debriefings may be available by phone as well. An individual will usually do debriefings on behalf of the team. The person conducting the debriefing is usually the lead person from the interview team.

When you ask for an interview debriefing, be very cautious. While you are likely to be extremely disappointed by the interview outcome, you want to continue to present yourself as someone who is eager to learn and willing to try again. Your positive attitude about your own future and your openness to professional growth will make you memorable and can support your next efforts in an interview. Your focus during the debriefing should always be on self-improvement in preparation for your next interview opportunity. Never ask for comparisons to other teacher candidates who were interviewed. This will show the person conducting the debriefing that you understand confidentiality issues and are focused on your growth and not on questioning the decisions of the interview team.

Another word of caution is needed here. Do not ask for a debriefing meeting at the interview. This may show a lack of confidence in your success. Wait until you have had a call about the outcome of your interview. At that time, you can ask whom you should contact if you are interested in a debriefing meeting. It is wise to make an appointment for a debriefing at a later date, rather than accepting a lengthened discussion during a results oriented call. This will give you time to think about pertinent questions and allow you to make detailed notes. After all, the feedback is only valuable if you use it to improve during your next opportunity.

Using Feedback from an Interview to Improve

If you have been invited to an interview, this demonstrates that the interview team is already impressed by you on a number of scores. They have seen your cover letter and are interested in what you have to offer to the advertised position and the potential you have to fit their school or board needs. They have seen your application and resume and have determined that you are fully qualified for the position that they have to offer.

During the interview, they are trying to get to know you in a comparative context. Your responses to each of their questions are being analyzed against their criteria or "look fors". Immediately after all of the interviews are completed, they will also try to compare what you can bring to the job to what other candidates have to offer.

As interviewers end their interview sessions with candidates, they will go through an individual process, followed by a committee process. In each process, they try to rank their overall impressions of each candidate for the position. Following their individual rankings, the interview team will usually discuss each person's ranking, trying to come to consensus, until they have identified the person they most prefer for the position. During this process, the interview committee will usually select a second or perhaps even a third person they would consider to be most suited to the job. At this point in their deliberations, they are referring to their personal interview notes and using examples of things you said in the interview to support your candidacy. This is why it is so important for you to remember to focus everything you say in the interview on ensuring that you have shown you are a good fit for the school, the job, the system, the team you will work with, and the supervisor.

Ranks and Positions

Most teacher applicants apply to several school boards and may even apply for international teaching positions. It is often wise to go to as many interviews as you are offered before you make final decisions about accepting a job. Sometimes, the board's hiring timelines will not allow you the day or two you may want to consider your options after the interviews are complete. But, if that time is available, it is wise to take advantage of it to ensure that you are happy with your decision.

This is one of the reasons why hiring teams will typically rank several applicants for a position in their order of preference. It is not uncommon for their top ranked applicant to also be offered a job by another school board. When that happens, hiring teams will revisit their lists and offer the job to their second selection. Since this person is already deemed to be qualified and suitable for the position, the ranking process saves time for the interviewers and recognizes that there are only very small differences among candidates who have received top rankings by the interviewers. It should not be considered to be a slight or an insult if you are offered the job after someone else has accepted one elsewhere and turned this one down. It was probably a very closely contested top ranking in the first place.

Professional Ethics and Accepting Teaching Positions

It has long been standard practice in the teaching profession to consider a verbal job acceptance to be binding. Since interviewers put time and effort into the process and try to be fair and sensitive to teacher candidates, they expect the same consideration. If you are contacted after an interview and offered a job and accept it, that is legally and ethically binding on you.

However, it does happen that some highly suited teacher candidates may be offered a job, accept it verbally, then have another imminent job offer, which they prefer. If a candidate does reverse their decision and later refuse a job offer that they initially accepted verbally, it can leave a trail of decisions within the school board that need to be revisited. However, because schools would prefer to have happy employees, they will most likely agree to allow you to accept the alternative position. Just be aware this is not a popular practice and can make it difficult for you to reapply to the first board in the future if you ever want that option.

Accepting a Job Offer

If a job is offered to you, and you accept it, there are a number of things you need to clarify immediately. These include:

- the status of the position (occasional teacher contract or permanent teacher contract)
- the conditions of the contract (full time, part time, percentage)
- location(s) of the position, if known
- scheduling of the contract if it is less than a full contract (i.e., Is it for mornings, afternoons, alternate days, etc.?)
- people you should contact to discuss the position
- duties and responsibilities of the job

For some of these details, you can ask the person who has called to offer you the job. Others will need to be directed to the school administration or the board's Human Resources department. However, you should ensure that shortly after accepting a contract verbally, you have received a letter stating the exact conditions and terms of your employment. This can take some time since board personnel will have to check all of your application documents and provide documentation to various departments within the board and the relevant union, but it is your responsibility to follow up and make sure you receive written confirmation of the employment offer.

Shortly after you receive a contract or an occasional position you will be contacted by your union with information about your rights and responsibilities. In some jurisdictions, the unions are different for the teachers on contract and the teachers on occasional supply teacher lists. You should make yourself aware of the services provided for you by your union. These sometimes include valuable professional development opportunities that will enrich your growth in the profession. Every teacher's union provides the option to communicate with members by phone or through the internet. Therefore, it would be valuable to become aware of how to contact your union representatives, using these approaches, as soon as you are hired. A union contact person can provide some guidance for you if you have employment questions as you enter the profession.

Contracts and Collective Agreements

It is important to understand the differences between teaching contracts and collective agreements. Both of these define your conditions of employment but in different ways.

A contract defines when, where, and for whom you will work. The collective agreement is negotiated with your board to define how you will be compensated for the work you do, and other details of your employment not addressed in your contract (e.g., pay schedules, allowances, benefits, grievance procedures, etc.). It is your responsibility to know the terms of both your contract with the board and your collective agreement as negotiated by your union. You should acquire documents that outline both of these sets of requirements as soon as possible after accepting a contract.

Starting the New Teaching Job

If you have been successful with getting the teaching job or supply list placement that you want to start your career, you are on your way to an exciting and rewarding career. You already know from your practice teaching experience that the job of teaching is very demanding, with the rewards of seeing young people grow and learn being the main aspect of the job that can energize and sustain you.

As you start into this new role, it will be helpful if you can find a confidential mentor who agrees to offer you advice and guidance during your first year or so in the role of teacher. As you consider approaching a colleague to mentor you, be careful to select a colleague whose professional practice is widely admired in the school and among your colleagues. Select someone who is positive in their approach to problems and kind to other adults and the children they serve.

In this mentor relationship you could investigate the possibility of developing an intense mentoring that includes discussions of practice, theories behind the practice, observation of your practice followed by feedback from your mentor and further observed practice. This is the ideal professional relationship to help you grow in your teaching role and guide you toward optimal development as a professional.

Summary

This book is intended to help you prepare for an interview to acquire a teaching job. You are well prepared for your career as a teacher. Being prepared for the interview will help you ensure that you get an opportunity to work in the classroom as soon as possible.

By reading and reflecting on the messages in this book you have learned that there are 10 critical things to review to help you prepare for a teaching interview. These include:

- know the process that school boards use to have potential teachers apply for available teaching jobs;
- prepare the paper work that is required to support your job application;
- dress professionally for your interview;
- find out who will interview you so that you can consider their perspectives as you address answers to their interview questions;
- focus on making a strong first impression as you enter the interview room;
- learn how interviews are typically structured so you can plan for key questions;
- anticipate the questions to help you prepare scenarios on which to structure your answers;
- structure your responses to the interview questions;
- take control of the end of your interview to leave a strong impression; and

- understand what happens and should happen after your interview so that the interview process itself is a learning experience for you.

As you enter this demanding and rewarding profession we wish you luck and fulfillment. You have the knowledge and skills to challenge and change the world through your teaching.

REFERENCES

Anderson, N., Lievens, F., van Dam, K., & Ryan, A. (2004). Future perspectives on employee selection: Key directions for future research and practice. *Applied Psychology: An International Review, 53,* 487-501.

Antonioni, D., & Park, H. (2001). The effect of personality on peer ratings of contextual work behaviours. *Personnel Psychology, 54*, 331-360.

Bill and Melinda Gates Foundation. (2010). *Learning about teaching: Initial findings from the Measures of Effective Teaching Project.* Retrieved from www.gatesfoundation.org/ . . . / preliminary-findings-research-paper.pdf

Boyd, D., Goldhaber, D. D., Lankford, H. & Wyckoff, J. H. (2007). The effect of certification and preparation on teacher quality. *The Future of Children, 17*, 45-68. Retrieved from *http://muse.jhu. edu*

Campbell R. J., Kyriakides, L., Muijs, R. D., & Robinson, W. (2003). Differential teacher effectiveness: Towards a model of research and teacher appraisal. *Oxford Review of Education*, *29*, 347-362.

Cashin, W. E. (1994). Student ratings of teaching: A summary of the research. In K. A.

Feldman and M. B. Paulsen (Eds.), *Teaching and learning in the college classroom* (pp. 531-541). Needham Heights, MA: Simon and Schuster.

Cochran-Smith, M., & Power, C. (2010). New directions for teacher preparation. *Educational Leadership, 67*(8), 6-13.

Council of Ministers of Education, Canada, n.d. Agreement-n-principle: Labour mobility chapter of the agreement on international trade/teaching profession. *www. cmec.ca/else/agreement.stm*

Cranston, J. (2012). Exploring school principals' hiring decisions: Fitting in and getting hired. *Canadian Journal of Educational Administration and Policy, 135.*

Darling-Hammond, L. (1997). *Doing what matters most: Investigations in quality teaching.* New York: National Commission on Teaching and America's Future, Teachers College, Columbia University.

Darling-Hammond, L. (2001). The challenge of staffing our schools. *Educational Leadership, 58*(8), 12-17.

Darling-Hammond, L. (2003). Keeping good teachers: Why it matters, what teachers can do. *Educational Leadership, 60*(8), 6-13.

Darling-Hammond, L., & Berry, B. (1999). Recruiting teachers for the 21st century: The foundation for educational equity. *Journal of Negro Education, 68,* 254-279.

DeArmond, M., Gross, B., & Goldhaber, D. (2010). Is it better to be good or lucky? Decentralized teacher selection in 10 elementary schools. *Educational Administration Quarterly, 46,* 322-362.

Dedyna, K., (2011). Teaching grads face slim prospects in crowded job market. *The Times Colonist,* June 13. *http://www. vancouversun.com/story_print.html?id=4937804&sponsor=*

Dehaas, J., (2011). Two-thirds of new teachers can't find full-time work. Macleans OnCampus, June 15. *http://oncmapus. macleans.ca/education/2011/06/15/two-thirds-of-new-teachers-can't-find-full-time-work/comment-page-1/*

Dinham, S., Ingvarson, L., & Kleinhenz, E. (2008). Teaching talent: The best teachers for Australia's classrooms. *Teaching standards and teacher evaluation.* Retrieved from http:// research.acer.edu.au/teaching_standards.12

Ehrhart, K. H. & Makransky, G. (2007). Testing vocational interests and personality as predictors of person-vocation and person-job fit. *Journal of Career Assessment, 15,*206-226.

Firestone, W. A., & Louis, K. S. (1999). Schools as cultures. In J. Murphy & K. S. Louis (Eds.), *Handbook of research on educational administration* (2nd ed., pp.297-322). San Francisco: Jossey-Bass.

Fullan, M. (2011). *Choosing the wrong drivers for whole system reform* (Seminar Series paper No. 204). East Melbourne, AU: Centre for Strategic Education. Retrieved from www. cse.edu.au

Gladwell, M. (2008, December 15). Most likely to succeed. *The New Yorker.* Retrieved from *www.newyorker.com/ reporting/2008/12/15121fa_fact_gladwell*

Goldhaber, D., & Hansen, M. (2010). Using performance on the job to inform teacher tenure decisions. *American Econonic Review: Papers and Proceedings, 100,* 250-255. Retrieved from www. aea.org/articles.php?doi=10.1257/aer.100.2.250

Harris, D. N. (2004). Putting a high-quality teacher in every Florida classroom: Policy brief. Retrieved from *www.nepc.colorado. edu/files/EPSL_0404-111-EPRU.pdf*

Harris, D. N., Rutledge, S. A., Ingle, W. K., & Thompson, C. C. (2007). *Mix and match: What principals look for when hiring teachers and what it means for teacher quality policies.* Retrieved from *www.teacherqualityresearch.org/mix_match.pdf*

Henry, G. T., Bastian, K. C., & Fortner, C. K. (2011). Stayers and leavers: Early-career teacher effectiveness and attrition. *Educational Researcher 40*(6), 271-280.

Herriot, P. (1989). *Recruitment in the 1990s.* London: Institute of Personnel Management.

Jacob, B., & Lefgren, L., (2006). When principals rate teachers. *Education Next, 6*(2), 59-64. Retrieved from www. Educationnext.org/journal/spring06/

Karren, R. J., & Graves, L. M. (1994). Assessing person-organization fit in personnel selection: Guidelines for future research. *International Journal of selection and Assessment, 2,* 146-156.

Kristof-Brown, A. L., Zimmerman, R. D., & Johnson, E. C. (2005). Consequences of individuals' fit at work: A meta-analysis of person-job, person-organization, person-groups and person-supervisor fit. *Personal Psychology, 58,* 281-342.

Little, O., Goe, L., & Bell, C. (2009). *A practical guide to evaluating teacher effectiveness.* Washington, DC: National Comprehensive Center for Teacher Quality. Retrieved from *www.tqsource.oeg/ publications/practicalGuide.pdf*

Maynes, N., & Hatt, B. (2012). Hiring and Supporting New Teachers who Focus on Students' Learning. *Canadian Journal of Educational Administration and Policy.*

Montgomery, C. (1996). Organization fit is key to job success. *HR Magazine, 41*(1), 94-97.

Ontario College of Teachers. (2011). *Transition to teaching 2010: Early-career teachers in Ontario schools.* Toronto: Ontario College of Teachers. Retrieved from *www.oct.ca*

Organization for Economic Cooperation and Development (OECD). (2004, February). The quality of the teaching workforce: Policy brief. *OECD Observer.* Retrieved from *www.oecd.org/ dataoecd/17/9/29478720.pdf*

Organization for Economic Cooperation and Development (OECD). (2005). *Teachers matter: Attracting, developing and retaining effective teachers.* Paris: OECD.

Pappano, L. (2011). Using research to predict great teachers. *Harvard Education Letter 27*(3).

Plumbley, P. (1985). *Recruitment and selection,* (4th ed.). London: Institute of Personnel Management.

Rabowinski, W., & Travers, R. M. W. (1953). Problems of defining and assessing teacher effectiveness. *Educational Theory, 3,* 212-219.

Rivkin, S. J., Hanushek,E. A., & Kain, J. F. (2005). Teachers, schools, and academic achievement. *Econometrica, 73,* 417-458. Retrieved from www.economics.harvard.edu/ . . . HanushekRivkinKain

Schultz, T. W. (1961). Investment in human capital. *American Economic Review, 51,* 1-16.

Sekiguchi, T. (2004). Person-organization fit and person-job fit in employee selection: A review of the literature. *Osaka Keidai Ronshu, 54*(6), 179-196.

Walsh, K., & Tracy, C. O. (2004). *Increasing the odds: How good policies can yield better teachers.* Washington, DC: National Council on Teacher Quality.

Wise, A. E., Darling-Hammond, L., & Berry, B. (1987). *Effective teacher selection: From recruitment to retention.* CA: Santa Monica, RAND.

Young, J., Levin, B., & Wallin, D. W. (2007). *Understanding Canadian schools: An introduction to educational administration* (4th ed.). Toronto: Nelson.

Zhu, C. J., & Dowling, P. J. (2002). Staffing practices in transition: Some empirical evidence from China. *International Journal of Human Resource Management, 13*, 569-597.

APPENDIX

From various sources across Canada, a variety of questions that have been asked during teaching interviews are provided here. You are reminded that the specific questions that will be asked during an interview are designed by the school jurisdiction or by the interview team to reflect their current interests and needs for an appropriate fit. However, this may provide some support as you prepare specific details related to topics for your interview.

Review Chapters 7 to 10 to prepare both topics and structured responses for your interview.

The following sample questions are sorted in the following pages using the framework that was outlined in Chapter 7. This includes the categories of:

- Commitment to pupils and pupil learning;
- Leadership and community;
- Ongoing professional learning;
- Professional knowledge, including planning, implementing, and assessing; and
- Management and communication practices.

Since many questions that have been asked during local interviews from many jurisdictions are not formulated as performance-based questions, the samples provided below are shown as both actual wording and as performance-based adaptations of the questions.

Sample Questions

Commitment to Pupils and Pupil Learning

Crystal Ball Question Sample	Performance Based Question Sample
What is your personal philosophy of teaching?	Tell us about how you have applied your philosophy of teaching to create engaging learning in your classroom experiences.
What role have initiatives in literacy, numeracy and special education had in your classroom?	Tell us about how you have addressed the implementation of new initiatives in literacy, numeracy, and special education in your teaching.
How would you address a situation where a student did not demonstrate commitment to the Catholic faith?	Tell us about a time when you faced a situation where you realized that a student did not feel committed to the Catholic faith.
What distinguishes you from the other candidates?	Tell us about how you have experienced your unique skills and qualities in your professional practice.
How are you going to handle stress of this job?	Tell us about a time when you realized how stressful the role of teacher can be.
What do you have to offer to the school?	Tell us about a time when you have been able to provide complementary support to a teaching staff because of the unique set of skills you have to offer.
Why do you want to teach?	Tell us about when you realized that teaching was the career you wanted to pursue.
How are you going to manage a classroom with students (more than 1) on IEPs?	Tell us how you have managed the needs of students in a classroom where several students had IEPs.
How will you plan learning for a gifted child in your classroom?	Tell us about a time when you taught to meet the learning needs of a gifted child.

TEN THINGS YOU NEED TO KNOW BEFORE YOU INTERVIEW FOR A TEACHING JOB   137

What does it mean to you to be a transformative teacher?	Tell us about a time when your approach to teaching was transformative.
Discuss some IEP accommodations you have used in your classroom.	Tell us about the IEP accommodations or modification you routinely use in your teaching.
What are your thoughts on Bill XXX?	Tell how the recent legislation about XXX has influenced your teaching.
What is your contingency plan when you are not well prepared for a lesson?	Tell us about a time when the lesson you were teaching was not going well and you had to move to a contingency plan to ensure learning.
How will you address modifications and accommodations in French?	Tell us how you have addressed program accommodations and modifications when teaching French.
How do you feel about a French only classroom?	Tell us about the positives and negatives you have encountered in teaching in a French only classroom.
How do you measure student success and know that your students are successful?	Tell us how you have measured students' success as you teach.
What are the most important characteristics of an effective music teacher?	Tell us about how you have made teaching music effective in a classroom.

Leadership and Community

Crystal Ball Question Sample	Performance Based Question Sample
Define your Catholicity.	Tell us about how you have used your Catholic faith in your classroom teaching.
How would you demonstrate your Catholic Faith in your Parish and in you classroom? OR How would I know that I am walking into a Catholic Classroom when I walk into yours? OR What are the differences between Catholic and Public school boards?	Tell us about how you have incorporated demonstrations of your Catholic faith into your classroom and your community.
Why are you interested in teaching with this board?	Tell us about how you have integrated into this community and have invested in the mission of this school board.
What does the term collegiality mean to you?	Tell us about a time when you have worked on a collaborative or collegial professional effort with colleagues.
How would you deal with a problematic situation that has arisen between you and a colleague?	Tell us about how you have dealt with a problematic situation that has arisen between you and a colleague.
How would you respond to a student's disclosure of any form of abuse?	Tell us about a time when a student disclosed some form of neglect or abuse to you.
What is your homework policy?	Tell us about how you have developed, communicated, and managed your homework policy in your classroom.

What are your thoughts on team-teaching?	Tell us about a time when you engaged in a team teaching situation.
What will your Language Arts program look like?	Tell us about a time when you were responsible for teaching the entire Language Arts program.
What will your Mathematics program look like? OR What does hands on mathematics look like to you?	Tell us about a time when you were responsible for teaching the entire Mathematics program.
What questions will you consider when you are creating a unit plan?	Tell us about the questions or issues you have considered when you have developed a unit plan.
How are you going to work with a culturally diverse community?	Tell us about how you have planned for instruction and communication in a culturally diverse community.
Why do you want to teach in a First Nations community?	Tell us about your beliefs about First Nations education that reflect your past experience with this group of students.

Ongoing Professional Learning

Crystal Ball Question Sample	Performance Based Question Sample
What are some of your professional strengths and weaknesses?	Tell us about how you have used your professional strengths to inform your teaching and how you have addressed any weaknesses to improve your professional practice.
What was the best lesson you ever taught?	Tell us about an effective lesson you have taught.
What is your 5 year professional plan for your growth?	Tell us about how you have addressed your own professional growth since focusing on teaching as a career and what your plans are for continuing this growth.
What does the phrase "teacher as learner" mean to you?	Tell us about a time when you found yourself in a situation where you were learning along with your students.
How are you going to demonstrate to your students that you are a life long learner?	Tell us about a time when you engaged in co-learning with a student.
Reflect on the most difficult challenge you had on a practicum. What was it? How did you adapt?	Tell us about how you handled a difficult situation on a practicum.
How will you keep yourself current as an occasional teacher?	Tell us about how you have upgraded your professional knowledge.
What life experience do you bring to a First Nations community? OR How will you cope living in a First Native's community without many conveniences that we have taken for granted?	Tell us about your experience teaching in a First Nations community.
How can Professional Learning Communities (PLCs) enhance your students' learning?	Tell us about your experience with learning new strategies from colleagues through PLCs or Communities of Learners approaches.

Professional Knowledge

Crystal Ball Question Sample	Performance Based Question Sample
What is an entrance plan?	Tell us about a time when you started a new job where you had responsibility for a group. Explain how you formed an entrance plan before you started this job.
What was the worst lesson that you taught? Why? How would you change it?	Tell us about a lesson you taught that was not as effective as you would have liked. Explain why the lesson was not fully effective and what you did in the next lesson to improve.
Select a unit of study, that you were responsible for planning and implementing and explain how you addressed specific student needs.	Tell us how you have designed units of study to address specific student needs.
How would you address cultural diversity in the school and community?	Tell us about how you have addressed issues of cultural diversity in your school and the school's community.
What does success mean in your classroom?	Tell us about a time when you did something in your teaching that ensured the success of a student who was struggling with new learning.
How would you integrate technology into your lessons?	Tell us about a lesson or unit you have taught where engagement was stronger because of how you integrated technology into your lesson or unit.
How would you use assessment, report card data, and EQAO results to make decisions to improve your teaching?	Tell us how you have used various forms of student achievement data to improve your teaching.
What are diagnostic, formative, and summative assessments?	Tell us how you have used various forms and uses of assessment to inform your professional decisions in the classroom.

How are you going to encourage students to demonstrate their knowledge in different ways?	Tell us about how you have encouraged students to use different ways to demonstrate their knowledge.
How would you use backward design principles in your teaching?	Tell us how you have used backward design principles in your professional role.
How would you provide balanced literacy and cross curricular learning in your classroom?	Tell us about a lesson or unit that you have designed to provide balanced literacy and cross-curricular or integrated learning in your classroom.
How are you going to motivate reluctant learners in your classroom?	Tell us about a time when you found that a student was not engaged in the learning.
Talk to me about your teaching portfolio.	Tell us about the unique evidence of your professional skills and practices that you have included in your teaching portfolio.
How would you address split-level or combined grade classes?	Tell us how you have used specific strategies of universal design for instruction to address teaching in a combined grade class.
What does enduring understanding mean to you?	Tell us about a time when you have planned a unit to ensure the achievement of enduring understandings as outlined in a curriculum guideline.
What does authentic assessment mean to you?	Tell us about a time when you have used authentic assessment in your classroom.
What are the differences between learning skills and subject specific assessment?	Tell us about how you have addressed instruction and assessment of learning skills in your teaching.
Why you feel suited for this position?	Tell us about the experience, qualifications, and beliefs that make you the most suitable candidate for this position.

How are you going to use assessment exemplars?	Tell us about a time in your teaching when you have used assessment exemplars effectively.
How are you going to incorporate the main concepts of the *Growing Success* document into your classroom?	Tell us about how you have adapted and improved your assessment and evaluation practices to reflect current legislation calling for improvement in this area (e.g., *Growing Success*).
How would you address differentiated instruction?	Tell us how you have addressed differentiated instruction and differentiated assessment in your classroom.
What kind of work has prepared you to be a supply teacher? OR Identify three challenges that an occasional teacher may face on any given assignment.	Tell us about what you have done to prepare you for the challenge of becoming a supply teacher.
What are SMART goals?	Tell us about how you have used curriculum guidelines to start the process of setting learning goals for a series of lessons (e.g., using SMART goals).
You have been called for supply work. What kind of questions will you ask upon arrival at school?	Tell us about the background knowledge you try to acquire when you have arrived at a school for a new supply teaching assignment.
What are your responsibilities at the end of a supply day?	Tell us about what you have done to support the regular classroom teacher's return at the end of a supply teaching assignment.
What does inclusion mean to you? OR What does culturally responsive teaching mean to you? OR What is your idea of land-based learning?	Tell us about sample strategies you have used in your teaching to ensure that you have engaged students in inclusive and culturally responsive learning experiences.

How are you going to motive reluctant learners? What strategies could you use?	Tell use about strategies you have used effectively to engage reluctant learners.
What does the Teachers' Code of Ethics mean to you?	Tell us about a situation where you had to rely on the professional Code of Ethics to guide your decisions in a difficult situation with another teacher.
Spirituality is important in the First Nations culture. How would you promote it in your classroom?	Tell us about how you have promoted awareness of the importance of spirituality in First Nations cultures in your teaching.
Some students may not speak English very often at home. How would you accommodate those students who may not be fluent in the language of instruction in the classroom?	Tell us about how you have accommodated and adapted your strategies to support communication of students who may not be fluent in the language of instruction in your classroom.
Do you enjoy teaching and learning outdoors?	Tell us about how you have used the natural environment to engage the cultural interests of your students.
What will make you a good French (or other language) teacher?	Tell us about the successes you have had teaching this language.
Describe the programs and teaching methods you will use to teach each strand of the French program.	Tell us about the program and strategies you have used to teach French.
How will you use Bloom's Taxonomy as a French Teacher?	Tell us how you have applied Bloom's Taxonomy to design instruction in French.

Management and Communication Practices

Crystal Ball Question Sample	Performance Based Question Sample
Explain your classroom management plan.	Tell us about how your written classroom management plan has been applied to a situation in a classroom.
How would your colleagues describe you?	Tell us about a time when you worked with another colleague on a cooperative professional task.
Explain how you would nurture good relationships with the parents of your students?	Tell us about how you have addressed a concern expressed by a parent.
How will you ensure that your classroom provides a safe and structured environment?	Tell us about how you have applied your classroom management skills to create a safe and structured learning environment when you have taught.
How would you deal with an irate parent?	Tell us about a time when you dealt with an irate parent.
How will you manage a situation where a student uses inappropriate language or inappropriate behaviour?	Tell us about a time when you had to address a student's inappropriate language or inappropriate behaviour.
What is your classroom management plan?	Tell us about how you have used proactive and reactive classroom management approaches in your teaching.
What will you do if you show up at a school for a supply teaching assignment and you find that no lesson plans have been left for you?	Tell us about how you have created a successful learning day when you have arrived in a new supply assignment and found that no lesson plans have been left for you.
What do you do to prepare for a new supply teaching assignment?	Tell us about a time when you prepared effectively to ensure a good day of teaching.
What sort of issues do you believe will be seen in a First Nation's classroom?	Tell us about two or three examples of issues you have addressed while working with First Nations students.

How will you involve the community and parents in your classroom?	Tell us about how you have involved the community and parents in your classroom.
What are you going to do to prepare for the teaching position ahead of the arrival of students?	Tell us about what you have done to prepare a classroom ahead of students' arrival.
How do you help students develop a passion for learning another language?	Tell us about how you have helped students develop a passion for learning another language.
How would you handle a student or parent who communicates orally or in writing that French is not important?	Tell us about a time when you have had to speak to a student or parent about the value of learning French.
How would you handle the responsibility or the challenges of being a French Teacher for teaching multiple grades and classes and having to transition from room to room?	Tell us how you have managed the challenges of being a rotary French teacher responsible for the French program in many grades.

Note: It is common for second language postings to include both oral and written aspects in the interview process. These parts of the interview may be conducted at the same time as the face-to-face interview or may be scheduled as separate components of the interview and some aspects may be conducted by phone.

Lightning Source UK Ltd.
Milton Keynes UK
UKOW02f1203220816

281215UK00003B/801/P